# A TASTE

......................... OF .........................

# *adventure*

## A COLLECTION OF RECIPES
## FROM AROUND THE WORLD

EBURY
PRESS

# Contents

# Welcome to
# *Our World*

*Food is not simply fuel. It's an excuse for friends, old and new, to gather together; a celebration of regional idiosyncrasies and specialities. It is part of our cultural identity.*

One of the great joys of travelling is being able to pull up a chair and break bread with the locals, seeing where the ingredients are sourced and even learning a traditional recipe or two. It is, quite literally, the best way to get a taste of a destination.

What better way to bring a little bit of adventure into your home than with a recipe inspired by travel? Whether you're a hiker hoping for a hunger-defeating feast, a streamlined cyclist searching for a snack, or a seasoned traveller wanting to recreate that rooftop mojito moment with friends, finding ways to fit those flavours back into your daily routine will always remind you of your travels.

This globetrotting recipe book is packed with exciting ways you can recreate your adventures in your own kitchen. Inside these pages you'll find authentic recipes from Italian brothers, Vietnamese restauranteurs, Exodus staff members, knowledgeable leaders and, of course, our wonderful travellers.

So as with all adventures, it's time to dive right in. Join us for the journey.

**ⓔ exodus*travels***

# ⓔ exodus*travels*

# A TASTE OF ADVENTURE

*It all began in 1974 with two men and one dream:*
*The desire to travel to far-flung parts of the world,*
*interact with local people and learn more about the*
*amazing planet we all share.*

Back then it was 21-week overland expeditions on huge, rugged 12-ton trucks headed on the hippie trail to Kathmandu and beyond. Veteran overland leaders will happily spend hours swapping stories of disasters on the road, of trips that overran in length by five weeks, of being ambushed in Sudan on Christmas Day and various versions of getting mired in mud. All whilst being fuelled by butterscotch Angel Delight.

The world has changed a lot over the years. Nobody back then had smartphones, DSLR cameras or worried about the WiFi password – even the fax machine was yet to be invented. It's fair to say that since then Exodus has grown up a bit too, and our definition of adventure has evolved with us. But one thing that has never changed is our vision and passion for travel. Put simply, it's in our DNA.

So, how do we do things now? Well, a great holiday is like a great meal, it starts with good – quality ingredients – and certainly doesn't feature powdered desserts!

We seek out new and interesting destinations, or find an innovative way to rediscover somewhere we know well. We start by combing the different highlights of a region – architectural masterpieces, scenic viewpoints, historic hotspots. To this we add a generous dollop of local knowledge from our award-winning guides, carefully crafting our timings to avoid the crowds. Then we throw in a dash of activity – from gentle walking to iconic treks, easy riverside cycling to hardcore ascents, kayaking, canyoning, or just meandering around the local market. Finally we season liberally with off-the-beaten-track touches – the best back-alley gelateria, the secret garden most people miss, or the quirky little shrine that doesn't get mentioned in guidebooks.

We don't spectate, we participate – whilst always being mindful of the impact we have on the places we visit. When you travel with us, you get a taste of authentic travel. It could be staying the night in a historic Japanese ryokan, a Mekong Delta homestay, or a 16th-century castle in rural Catalonia. It could be meeting a local artisan cheesemaker in the Bosnian mountains, visiting a woman's argan oil cooperative in Morocco, or dancing the night away in a tiny Cuban taverna: it's about real insight into a culture, away from the main tourist drag, and giving you opportunities and memories you wouldn't find elsewhere.

These are carefully crafted adventures that take you away from the ordinary and into the extraordinary, enabling real immersion into a new culture and, of course, cuisine.

# Your Adventure, Your Way...

You choose how you travel. We've got all bases covered, regardless of how you like to approach things. Join a small group of like-minded travellers to share your experiences, get your own group together on an exclusive private adventure for just you and your loved ones, or strike out on your own self-guided escape, knowing Exodus have got your back every step of the way. Opt for a little extra luxury on a Premium Adventure. It's your adventure; you should have it your way.

You could be spotting your first wild jaguar (then your second, and third), trying tasty mozzarella straight from the factory in Italy, pushing yourself to your limits on the summit of Kilimanjaro or pedalling through aromatic pine forests towards panoramic views.

We've been creating unforgettable adventures for over 40 years, and now offer more than 500 itineraries to over 100 countries. All you have to do is decide which one is best for you.

*We we are very proud to say that 97% of our clients would recommend us to a friend.*

97% of our clients would **97%** recommend us to a friend

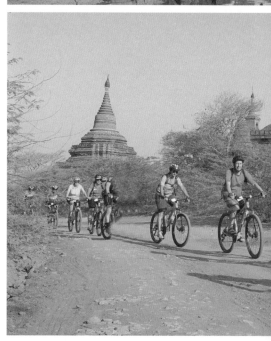

# Travelling Responsibly

Everywhere we visit is someone else's home; we always remember that, and treat it with respect.

'Tourism is one of the most important and largest industries on the planet. It employs more people worldwide than any other, with millions of families relying on tourism for their daily needs.' says our Managing Director, Peter Burrell.

We take our responsibility to these people seriously. Through sustainable, small-scale and small-group travel, we know we can have a positive impact on local economies and jobs, help preserve the environments, aid conservation efforts and pick sustainable options for our travellers. As well as being true to our ethos, we know this creates more interesting adventures for our customers.

Not only do we run our trips responsibly, but we also support a variety of charities, initiatives and projects across the globe. Just one example is the Nepal Earthquake Appeal, for which we won the *Sunday Times* Travel Editor's Award. Over 3,000 of our customers helped us raise more than £250,000 to aid those affected by the earthquakes of 2015, allowing us to make a real difference to many families.

One way we spent the money was funding a specialist medical camp in a remote Nepali village, where more than a thousand patients received treatment for a variety of long-standing conditions. 'It was incredible,' said our videographer Olly Pemberton, who travelled out from the UK to observe the camp. 'We were changing people's lives in front of my eyes.'

*'Tourism is one of the most important and largest industries on the planet.'*
– Peter Burrell, Exodus MD

## About This Book

This book aims to bridge the gap between adventure and our everyday life. It's a way for us to incorporate a little taste of the extraordinary into our normal day-to-day, to turn a meal into a trip down memory lane or a chance to branch out, to get a taste for somewhere new. So even when you're at home, you can send your taste buds travelling for you.

We've tailored the recipes to fit what you'll be able to find in the shops in the UK – we won't send you out to a Thai floating market hunting down obscure vegetables, but we haven't flinched away from some more adventurous recipes for the enthusiastic chef to relish either.

More than anything, though, it's about ways to celebrate the diverse and fantastic flavours from all around the world. We want to share those dishes with you, so you can share them with your friends, family and loved ones. After eating our way around the world for over forty years, with our knowledgeable leaders and lovely customers, we thought it was time to distil that knowledge into one place.

This cookbook is the result.

## @exodustravels

'I haven't been everywhere, but it's on my list.'
– Susan Sontag

*europe*

# dishes

# ĆEVAPI WITH AJVAR

## flatbreads filled with grilled meat & red pepper sauce

**SERVES 4** as a side

**PREPARE** 45 minutes (plus chilling and cooling) **COOKING** about 40 minutes

### ĆEVAPI

250g lean minced beef

250g minced pork

2 cloves of garlic, peeled and crushed

1tsp smoked paprika

1 egg, beaten

1 slice of bread, made into crumbs

### AJVAR

4 red peppers

1 aubergine

3 cloves of garlic, peeled and chopped

Juice of 1 lemon

2tbsp olive oil

Salt and freshly ground black pepper

### TO SERVE

1 onion, peeled and very finely chopped

1tbsp finely chopped flat leaf parsley

Juice of 1 lemon

4 flatbreads

Soured cream

Paprika, to dust

Pickled guindilla peppers

Lemon wedges

Considered a national dish in Bosnia and Herzegovina, the ćevapi are made from minced meat, which can be beef or pork or a mix of the two, and flavoured with paprika and garlic. The meat mixture is then shaped into fat sausages which are cooked on a griddle until brown. They are served on flatbreads with ajvar, a flame-coloured roasted red pepper sauce, and topped with pickled peppers and soured cream. Prepare the ćevapi ahead of time and chill them in the fridge for several hours or overnight before cooking, so they have time to firm up.

### METHOD

To make the ćevapi, mix the minced beef, pork, garlic and paprika together in a bowl. Stir in the egg and breadcrumbs until the mixture sticks together.

With damp hands, shape into 8 thick sausages. Put them on a plate in a single layer, cover with cling film and chill in the fridge for several hours or overnight.

To make the ajvar, line a grill rack with foil and lay the peppers and aubergine on it. Grill until the vegetables are scorched all over. Remove from the grill, wrap the foil around the vegetables, folding over the edges to make a tightly sealed parcel, and leave to cool. Once cold, open the foil, strip off the skin from the peppers and remove the stalk and seeds. Peel the aubergine and discard the stalk.

Put the peppers, aubergine, garlic, lemon juice and olive oil in a food processor and blend to a coarse purée. Season with salt and pepper.

Mix together the chopped onion, parsley and lemon juice and spoon into a small bowl. Cover with cling film and chill in the fridge until needed.

When ready to serve, heat a ridged grill pan until very hot and cook the ćevapi for 10–15 minutes until cooked through, turning them so they brown all over. Warm the flatbreads in the oven.

Heat the ajvar or leave it cold, as you prefer, and spread some over the warm flatbreads. Top each with two ćevapi, a spoonful of soured cream dusted with paprika, and some of the chopped onion mix. Accompany with pickled guindilla peppers and extra lemon wedges to squeeze over.

# BRESKVICE

## little peach cakes

| SERVES 20 | PREPARE 1 hour (plus chilling and cooling time)　COOKING 15 minutes |

**FOR THE CAKE MIXTURE**

150g unsalted butter, diced and softened

100g caster sugar

2 eggs, beaten

400g plain flour

¾tsp baking powder

3tbsp lemon juice

**FOR THE FILLING**

6tbsp peach jam

1tsp cocoa powder

2tbsp chopped toasted hazelnuts

1tbsp dark rum or milk

**TO DECORATE**

Yellow and red liquid food colourings

Caster or granulated sugar, for coating

These pretty little cakes are a great favourite in Croatia at gatherings for family and friends. They are a cross between a sponge and a cookie and are sandwiched with a peach jam, cocoa and rum filling. Little peach cakes are also popular in Italy where they have a custard filling flavoured with peach brandy and are known as *Tortine di pesche*.

METHOD

To make the cakes, beat the butter and sugar together in a mixing bowl until light and fluffy. Gradually beat in the eggs, adding a tablespoon of the flour to prevent the mixture curdling.

Sift in the rest of the flour with the baking powder and stir in with the lemon juice. Bring the mixture together with your hands, kneading it lightly until smooth. Wrap in cling film and chill in the fridge for 1 hour.

Line two baking sheets with baking parchment. Preheat the oven to 190°C (fan 170°C)/gas 5. Pull off small pieces of the cake mixture and roll them with your hands into 40 walnut-sized balls.

Divide the balls between the baking sheets and bake for 15 minutes or until they are lightly coloured underneath but not brown on top. Transfer them to a wire rack to cool and then carefully cut out the centre of the base of each cake using the point of a sharp knife. Crush the pieces you have removed into crumbs with a rolling pin and set aside to add to the filling.

To make the filling, mix together the peach jam, cocoa powder, hazelnuts and rum or milk until evenly combined and then stir in the crumbs. Set aside.

To decorate the cakes, dilute the yellow and red food colourings with a little cold water. Using a small soft paintbrush, brush a little yellow colour over the cake halves, followed by the red, blending the colours together to resemble the skin of fresh peaches.

Spread out caster or granulated sugar on a plate and roll the painted cake halves in it before the food colouring dries. Sandwich the cake halves together in pairs with the filling.

# KNEDLIKY
## bread dumplings

**SERVES 4**   **PREPARE** 15 minutes   **COOKING** 45 minutes

Serve these dumplings for dinner as an accompaniment
to roast pork and sauerkraut, washed down with a stein
of beer. Any leftovers can be served for breakfast the next
day as a new twist on scrambled eggs. Chop the leftover
dumplings into small pieces and pan-fry in butter until
golden. Add beaten eggs and milk and stir over the heat
until the eggs are scrambled and set.

### INGREDIENTS

1 egg

Salt and freshly ground
black  pepper

60ml milk

180g plain flour

½tsp baking powder

2 slices of white bread,
crusts  removed, and cut
into  small cubes

### METHOD

In a mixing bowl, whisk together the egg, seasoning
and milk.

Gradually sift in the flour and baking powder, stirring
until you have a smooth dough that is stiff enough to
hold its shape. When the flour has been added, mix
in the bread cubes.

Dampen a piece of muslin or a similar clean cloth.
Shape the dough into a neat sausage roughly 20cm
long and 4cm thick and roll it up in the cloth, tying
the ends with string like a  Christmas cracker.

Bring a large pan of water to the boil. Carefully
lower the roll into the water, cover the pan and boil
for 45 minutes.

Drain the roll from the pan, then remove the cloth
immediately to  avoid the dumplings turning soggy.
Cut the dumpling into 2cm  slices.

Serve hot with roast pork and sauerkraut.

# BRYNDZOVÉ HALUŠKY

## potato dumplings with bryndza cheese & bacon

**SERVES 2**

**PREPARE** 20 minutes   **COOKING** about 15 minutes

### INGREDIENTS

300g floury potatoes,  peeled

125g plain flour

1tsp salt

200g streaky bacon  lardons

125g bryndza or another  soft cheese

*Our Tip!*

Feta, cottage cheese or even a crumbly goat's cheese could be used instead of bryndza sheep's milk.

Exodus staff member Louis Millington returned from a trip to Slovakia with a new love for this comforting traditional dish. 'I loved sharing this with my family,' he says. Slovak food is hearty and in the rural countryside lots of meat is eaten, particularly pork, which is served with halušky – potato dumplings. They are also Slovakia's most famous dish. This version of the dumplings is made using local bryndza sheep's milk cheese. The traditional way to shape them is to push the dough through a special halušky press, but it can also be cut into small pieces with a knife.

### METHOD

Coarsely grate the potatoes into a bowl and stir in the flour and salt to make a dough, kneading it with your hands so it sticks together.

Dry fry the lardons until they are golden brown. Drain on a plate lined with  kitchen paper and keep warm in a low oven.

Bring a large pan of water to the boil. Cut the dough into small dumplings about 2cm long and drop them into the boiling water. Cook for a few minutes until they float, then drain.

Mix the dumplings with the cheese and spoon them into a serving dish. Top with the hot bacon and serve at once.

# BYREK MI SPINAQ

## Albanian spinach pie

**SERVES 4**

**PREPARE** 30 minutes   **COOKING** 50–55 minutes

### INGREDIENTS

500g young fresh spinach leaves

2tbsp olive oil

2 large onions, peeled and chopped

1 egg, beaten

125g full-fat soured cream

125g natural Greek yoghurt

1tbsp chopped fresh mint

¼tsp freshly grated nutmeg

Salt and freshly ground black pepper

12 sheets of filo pastry

125g butter, melted

Central Albania is rich and fertile so vegetables grow there in abundance. Farmers sell their produce every day in the local markets and this crisp-topped pie could be made with any combination of leafy green vegetables bought there. While Albanian cooks would probably make the filo dough themselves, we'd recommend you buy it ready prepared, unless you're feeling particularly adventurous!

### METHOD

Put the spinach leaves in a large pan, add 2 tablespoons of cold water and place over a medium heat. Cover the pan and cook until the leaves wilt. Drain, pat the leaves with kitchen paper to blot off any excess water and chop them coarsely.

Heat the oil in a pan and fry the onions until softened and golden.

Put the spinach, fried onions, beaten egg, soured cream, yoghurt, mint and nutmeg in a large bowl. Season and stir until the ingredients are evenly combined.

Preheat the oven to 200°C (fan 180°C)/gas 6. Unroll the sheets of filo onto the work surface and cover them with a sheet of cling film and a damp tea towel.

> see tip

Brush a shallow oven-proof dish, measuring roughly 20 x 25cm, with melted butter. Brush the top of one filo sheet with butter and lay it in the dish, pushing it down gently to cover the base and sides.

Layer five more filo sheets on top, brushing each one with melted butter. Spoon in the spinach mixture, spreading it out evenly. Layer the remaining six sheets of filo on top of the filling, brushing each one with melted butter.

Trim away excess filo with kitchen scissors and brush any remaining butter over the pie. Score the top layers of pastry in a diamond pattern with a sharp knife and bake the pie for 40–45 minutes or until golden brown and crisp.

**Our Tip!** Filo pastry is not difficult to use but needs careful handling so the wafer-thin sheets don't tear. They also dry out very quickly and become brittle, so keep the sheets you're not working with covered with cling film and a damp cloth.

# MOHNKUCHEN

## poppy seed cake

**SERVES 12**

**PREPARE** 45 minutes (plus rising time for dough)　**COOKING** about 1 hour

### DOUGH

400g strong white bread flour

7g sachet of fast-action yeast

40g caster sugar

1½tsp salt

25g unsalted butter, cut into small pieces

4tbsp milk

Approx 225ml tepid water

Oil, for greasing

### FILLING

175g black poppy seeds

175ml milk

30g unsalted butter

100g caster sugar

3tbsp plain flour

1tsp vanilla extract

### ICING

100g icing sugar

Approx 1tbsp lemon juice

Chopped glacé fruit
e.g. lemon peel, ginger

Our Austrian tour leader Bob Mason says the poppy seed cake served at the Hotel Wienerhof in Trins is a great favourite with travellers. 'We have complimentary tea and cake in the afternoon after our walks, both in winter and summer. The hotel cook, Arno, bakes all the cakes himself and Mohnkuchen quickly disappears as soon as it's on offer!'

In Austria there are almost as many recipes for this traditional cake as there are bakers but, of course, they all contain lots of poppy seeds. In the Tyrol the poppy seed filling is usually spooned into a pastry case, whereas this version rolls a sweet yeast dough around the filling.

### METHOD

For the dough, mix together the flour, yeast, sugar and salt in a large bowl and rub in the butter. Add the milk and enough water to mix to a soft dough. Knead the dough for 5 minutes until it is smooth and elastic. Cover and leave to rise until it has doubled in size.

For the filling, put the poppy seeds and milk in a pan and bring to the boil. Cook, stirring frequently, until all the milk has been absorbed. Stir in the butter and sugar. Cool and then stir in the flour and vanilla until combined.

Roll out the dough to a rectangle about 30.5 x 38cm. Stir the filling and, with one long side of the dough towards you, spread the filling over to within 2.5cm of the edges.

Dampen the far edge of the dough with a little water and roll it up from the bottom into a tight log. Oil a large ring mould and shape the rolled-up dough into a round, pinching the join together. Lift seam side down into the ring. Cover loosely with oiled cling film and leave in a warm place until doubled in size.

> see tip

Preheat the oven to 190°C (fan 170°C)/gas 5. Bake for 30–35 minutes until golden brown. Carefully turn out onto a wire rack and leave to cool.

For the icing, sift the icing sugar into a bowl and add enough lemon juice to mix into a thick icing that can be drizzled over the cake. Scatter with chopped glacé fruit and leave until the icing has set before serving.

*Our Tip!*
The dough ring is tricky to lift without it losing its shape so we recommend sliding a couple of fish slice utensils underneath to make it easier to slide into the mould.

# KJÖTSÚPA

## Icelandic lamb soup

**SERVES 8**

**PREPARE** 30 minutes    **COOKING** 2–2½ hours

### INGREDIENTS

3tbsp oil

600g leg or shoulder of lamb steaks, cut into 2.5cm pieces

2 medium carrots, chopped

1 swede, peeled and cut into 2.5cm chunks

3 large potatoes, peeled and cut into 2.5cm chunks

1 large leek, trimmed and sliced

2 cloves of garlic, peeled and finely chopped

100ml dry white wine

2 litres beef or lamb stock

Salt and freshly ground black pepper

3tbsp chopped fresh parsley

This hearty soup is just the thing to keep out the cold during Iceland's long winters. Made by simmering lamb and root vegetables in broth or stock until the meat is falling apart, the resulting soup is full of flavour, and is the ultimate comfort food.

### METHOD

Heat 2 tablespoons of the oil in a large stock or soup pan and brown the lamb in batches until the pieces are evenly browned. Drain the pieces from the pan as they brown and set them aside.

Lower the heat, add the remaining tablespoon of oil to the pan and fry the carrots, swede and potatoes for 5 minutes, stirring occasionally. Add the leek and garlic and fry for another minute or so.

Deglaze the pan with the white wine, letting it bubble for a couple of minutes, then pour in the stock and return the meat to the pan.

Bring to the boil, remove any fat on the surface and season with salt and pepper. Lower the heat under the pan, cover with a tight-fitting lid and simmer gently for 1½–2 hours or until the meat and vegetables are very tender.

Ladle into soup plates, scatter over the parsley, and serve with plenty of crusty bread.

# TIRAMISU
## coffee-flavoured dessert

| SERVES 2 | PREPARE 15 minutes |
|---|---|

The name of this classic Italian dessert translates as 'pick-me-up', due no doubt to the lavish amounts of caffeine and mascarpone it contains! Our recipe is from our local partners in Italy, the Acampora brothers. They own the Hotel Due Torri – a family run hotel in a small village just outside Positano and Amalfi. Travellers who visit them are taught how to make this treasured family recipe at the hotel, and often take the recipe home with them.

## INGREDIENTS

1 egg, separated

1 tbsp caster sugar

1 tsp vanilla extract

250g mascarpone cheese

175ml cold strong black coffee

1 tbsp coffee liqueur (Kahlua or Tia Maria)

About 10 Savoiardi biscuits (sponge fingers)

1 tbsp cocoa powder

Strawberries, sliced to decorate

## METHOD

Put the egg yolk, sugar and vanilla in a bowl and stir until smooth and creamy.

Add the mascarpone and mix until it is evenly combined with the other ingredients. In another bowl, whisk the egg white until standing in soft peaks, then fold this gently into the mascarpone mixture.

Pour the coffee into a shallow bowl and add the coffee liqueur. Dip the biscuits briefly in the coffee mixture so they absorb some of it but do not become so soggy they fall apart.

Starting with the dipped biscuits, arrange layers of biscuits and mascarpone in individual glass dishes or tumblers, trimming the biscuits to fit in neatly, if necessary.

Dust the tops with cocoa powder and chill for several hours in the fridge before serving topped with strawberries.

# CARNE DE PORCO À ALENTEJANA

## pork, Alentejo style

**SERVES 4**

**PREPARE** 30 minutes (plus marinating) **COOKING** 1 hour 15 minutes

### INGREDIENTS

225ml dry white wine

4 cloves of garlic, peeled and finely chopped

1tsp paprika

Salt and freshly ground black pepper

2 bay leaves

900g loin of pork, trimmed of fat and cut into 2.5cm pieces

Oil, for frying

4 medium potatoes, peeled, cut into 2.5cm chunks and boiled until just tender

1 large onion, peeled and finely chopped

1tsp tomato purée

700g clams in their shells

4tbsp chopped parsley

'My partner Chris, his son Ed, and I discovered this dish when we went on an Exodus family adventure to Portugal last year.

We were staying in Vilanova de Milfontes and I was a bit nervous that a 12-year-old wouldn't like the food. He soon proved me wrong by trying everything we ordered! One night we discovered this dish on the menu of a local restaurant. Ed surprised me by saying it was his favourite dish, so on our last night we just had to go back and order it again,' says Exodus staff member Gina Eckersley.

### METHOD

Mix together the white wine, garlic, paprika, salt, pepper and bay leaves in a large bowl.

Add the pork, turning the pieces over until coated. Cover the bowl with cling film and leave in the fridge to marinate for 6 hours or overnight.

Lift the pork from the marinade. Heat 2 tablespoons of oil in a large pan and fry the pork in batches until browned on all sides, removing one batch from the pan before adding the next.

Strain the marinade into the pan and return all the pork to it. Cover the pan and simmer for about 1 hour or until the meat is very tender and the cooking liquid has reduced a little.

When the pork is almost cooked, heat 2 tablespoons of oil in a large frying pan, add the potatoes and fry until golden brown.

Heat 2 tablespoons of oil in a third large pan, add the onion and fry until softened. Stir in the tomato purée and add a couple of tablespoons of the cooking liquid from the pork.

Add the clams, cover the pan and cook over a low heat for a few minutes until all the clam shells have opened. Discard any that stay tightly closed.

> see tip

Drain the potatoes and add to the pork. Serve the pork and potatoes with the clams spooned on top, sprinkled with chopped parsley.

*Our Tip!* Before cooking the clams, soak them in a bowl of cold water for 15-20 minutes to remove any salt water or sand trapped inside the shells.

# DIOTS DE SAVOIE

## Diot sausages with lentils & cream

**SERVES 4**

**PREPARE** 15 minutes    **COOKING** about 50 minutes

### INGREDIENTS

2tbsp oil

8 Diots de Savoie sausages

1 large onion, peeled and thinly sliced

8 small potatoes or 2 large potatoes, cut into chunks

400g can of Puy lentils or another type of lentil, drained and rinsed

100ml double cream or full-fat crème fraîche

Fresh thyme leaves and a dusting of paprika, to garnish

Our local partners in France, Carey and her husband Mark, serve this dish to all their Alpine visitors. 'This was one of the first dishes Mark cooked for me when we met in 2002. We were visiting Chamonix for the first time and had been skiing all day so needed something hearty. He said he'd cook me this local dish – it was delicious! We married in 2006 and now have two children. Mark still cooks it for us from time to time,' says Carey.

Mark advises 'Diot sausages are a speciality of the Savoie region of France where we are based. They are thicker and firmer than your average sausage and have a more powerful flavour. You should be able to buy them from specialist butchers, French markets or some online butchers.'

### METHOD

Heat the oil in a large frying pan and fry the sausages and onion over a low heat for about 15 minutes or until the sausages are browned all over and cooked through, and the onion has softened. Transfer to a roasting pan or shallow oven-proof dish.

Meanwhile, boil the potatoes until they are tender. Drain and add to the sausages and onions.

Spoon the lentils around the sausages and potatoes and pour over the cream or crème fraîche.

Preheat the oven to 170°C (fan 150°C)/gas 3. Cover the pan with foil and cook for 30–35 minutes until everything is piping hot and the flavours infuse into the cream. Serve at once with fresh thyme leaves scattered over and a light dusting of paprika.

# PAELLA

## chicken & seafood rice dish

| **SERVES 4** | **PREPARE** 30 minutes **COOKING** 50 minutes |

### INGREDIENTS

3tbsp olive oil

2 boneless chicken thighs, skinned or not, as you prefer

1 large onion, peeled and sliced

2 cloves of garlic, peeled and finely chopped

1 red pepper, deseeded and chopped

1tsp smoked paprika

50g chorizo, skinned and cut into small chunks

225g Bomba paella rice

600ml dry white wine and chicken stock in equal quantities

Pinch of saffron threads, soaked in a couple of tablespoons of hot water for 10 minutes

115g frozen peas

2tbsp pitted black olives

1tbsp capers

12 raw prawns, shelled but heads and tails left on

12 mussels in their shells

Salt and freshly ground black pepper

2tbsp chopped leaf coriander or flat leaf parsley, to garnish

This chicken and seafood paella is based on one cooked by the head chef at our beautifully converted farmhouse accommodation in Andalucia, the Cortijo Rosario. 'La paella' actually refers to the wide, two-handled pan used for cooking, rather than the dish itself. Originating from Valencia, where the local people cooked rice with whatever produce they had available – usually onions, tomatoes and snails – in a shallow pan. Another great dish for sharing with friends and family.

### METHOD

Heat the oil in a paella pan or large frying pan and brown the chicken thighs on both sides over a high heat. Drain from the pan and cut each thigh into three pieces. Set aside.

Lower the heat, add the onion to the pan and cook until softened. Add the garlic, red pepper, smoked paprika and chorizo and fry for 5 minutes, stirring occasionally.

Tip in the rice and stir until the grains are coated in the oil in the pan. Slowly pour in the wine and stock, add the saffron and its soaking water, and return the chicken to the pan, pushing the pieces down into the rice.

Cook for 15 minutes, stirring occasionally, until the rice is not quite tender and the grains have absorbed most of the cooking liquid.

Stir in the frozen peas, olives, capers and prawns and lay the mussels on top. Cover the pan and cook for a further 5 minutes or until the prawns have turned pink, the mussel shells have opened, and the rice is tender.

Season with salt and pepper, scatter over the chopped coriander or parsley and serve at once straight from the pan.

 *Our Tip!*  If you don't have a big enough lid, a metal baking sheet placed on top of the pan works well.

# EUROPE
*drinks*

# NORDIC GLÖGG
## mulled wine

**SERVES 8–10** | **PREPARE** 10 minutes (plus infusing time)

After a day spent cross-country skiing, or on a cold winter's night, Scandinavians like nothing better to keep out the chills than a steaming cup of glögg. This mulled red wine is infused with whole spices and orange zest and served warm, with maybe a slug of vodka or aquavit added at the end. This would be a perfect drink to serve at a festive party or gathering.

### INGREDIENTS

1 bottle of red wine

2 sticks of cinnamon

Small knob of root ginger, fresh or dried

2tsp green cardamom pods

12 whole cloves

1 star anise

Strips of fresh or dried orange peel

75g caster sugar

2tbsp raisins

Vodka or aquavit, optional

### METHOD

Pour the wine into a large saucepan and add all the spices and the orange peel.

Add the sugar and heat until bubbles appear on the surface of the wine, but don't let it boil. Remove the pan from the heat and leave the wine to infuse for 1 hour or longer.

When ready to serve, reheat the wine slowly until just below boiling. Divide the raisins between serving mugs and pour over the hot wine, adding a splash of vodka or aquavit first for an extra kick, if you wish. Strain out the spices and orange peel or leave a few pieces in each mug, as preferred.

*Our Tip!*     Don't let the wine boil hard or you'll drive off the alcohol!

# APEROL SPRITZ
## classic Italian aperitif

**SERVES 1**

**PREPARE** 5 minutes

Exodus staff member Marta Marinelli says, 'This drink originates from the Veneto, my native region in Italy, but it is now popular all over Italy and the world. The 'spritz' was allegedly born in the 1800s. One theory is the soldiers and merchants liked the local wine but found the alcohol content was higher than in the wines they were used to. They asked their hosts to add a splash of water to the wine and over the years this has evolved into the cocktail it is today, made with the addition of Aperol, a liquor flavoured with bitter orange, gentian, rhubarb and the bark of the cinchona tree, among other ingredients.'

**INGREDIENTS**

Ice cubes

3 parts Prosecco

2 parts Aperol

1 part soda water

Orange slices to serve

**METHOD**

Half fill a tumbler with ice cubes.

Pour in the Prosecco, followed by the Aperol and top up with a splash of soda.

Drop an orange slice or wedge into the glass and serve at once.

# FRAPPÉ
## Greek iced coffee

**SERVES 1**

**PREPARE** 5 minutes

When the weather is hot, Athenians cool down by leisurely sipping a frappé at a pavement café as they watch the world go by. Now you can do it.

**INGREDIENTS**

175ml cold water

1½–2tsp instant coffee granules

2tsp caster sugar, or to taste

Ice cubes

50ml cold milk

**METHOD**

Warm 3 tablespoons of the water in a small bowl in the microwave and stir in the coffee until the granules dissolve.

Leave to cool then pour into a liquidiser and add the sugar. Blend until the mixture is thick and frothy.

Put ice cubes into a tall glass and pour in the foam. Stir in the remaining water and the milk and serve at once. Drink with a straw.

# SIMA

## Finnish lemon soda

| MAKES approx 5 litres | PREPARE 15 minutes (plus standing time) |
| --- | --- |
| | FERMENTATION 2–5 days |

Glasses of this lightly fermented drink, which is similar to mead, are raised in Finland to the toast of 'kippis!' as part of their 'Vappu' – May Day – celebrations. Brown sugar gives the drink a darker colour than what most of us think of as lemonade; and raisins dropped into the bottle while it ferments add to its rich golden hue.

### INGREDIENTS

2 lemons

5 litres water

100g granulated sugar

100g soft light brown sugar

¼tsp fresh or dried yeast

Raisins

### METHOD

Peel off the zest from the lemons in strips using a potato peeler. Cut away the pith and discard it, and slice the flesh.

Bring the water to the boil in a large pan, add the lemon zest, lemon flesh and sugars, lower the heat and simmer until the sugars dissolve.

Cool until lukewarm, add the yeast and stir until dissolved. Cover the pan, leave to sit at room temperature for 24 hours and then strain.

Put a few raisins in each preserving bottle or jar, pour in the lemon liquid and seal tightly. Refrigerate for 2–5 days, opening occasionally to release the gases that build up. When the raisins float, the sima is ready to drink.

Serve it with or without the raisins, with extra slices of lemon, if liked.

# north africa
# & middle east

# dishes

# LAMB TAGINE
## with prunes & almonds

**SERVES 4**

**PREPARE** 25 minutes   **COOKING** 1 hour

### INGREDIENTS

2tbsp oil

2 large onions, peeled and sliced

½ red pepper, deseeded and chopped

4 cloves of garlic, peeled and finely chopped

1tbsp finely chopped root ginger

2tbsp chopped fresh coriander

1tbsp chopped fresh parsley

Pinch of saffron threads soaked in 1tbsp hot water for 10 minutes

600g boneless lamb, cut from the leg and cubed

About 600ml lamb stock

150g pitted prunes, halved

1tbsp clear honey

Toasted flaked almonds, to garnish

> see tip

Staff member Dan Jackson cooks this classic Moroccan dish in a tagine – 'what do you mean you don't own one?', he jokes – but adds that you can also use a big saucepan. Earthenware tagine dishes have unique conical lids that condense steam and return it to the dish during cooking, keeping the food moist. If you use a saucepan, you'll need to increase the amount of stock you add as it will evaporate.

### METHOD

Heat the oil in a tagine and fry the onions, red pepper and garlic until softened.

Add the ginger, half the coriander, and the parsley, stir well and then add the saffron plus its soaking water and the lamb. Fry over a low heat for 5 minutes and then pour in enough stock to cover the meat.

Put the funnel-shaped lid on the tagine and leave to cook over a low heat for 40 minutes.

Add the prunes and honey, cook for 5 more minutes and serve sprinkled with the remaining coriander and the toasted almonds.

*Our Tip!* Dan suggests serving the lamb tagine with couscous to which Moroccans usually add carrots, courgettes and turnips to jazz it up a little. If prunes don't do it for you, he recommends you try apricots.

# MANSAF

## traditional lamb & yoghurt dish

**SERVES 4**

**PREPARE** 30 minutes  **COOKING** 2 hours

### INGREDIENTS

1kg lean lamb from the leg, cut into 2.5cm cubes

3tbsp oil, or samna or ghee (clarified butter)

1 large onion, peeled and finely chopped

1tsp ground coriander

1tsp ground cumin

1tsp ground cardamom

600ml lamb stock

500g jameed or natural Greek yoghurt

1 egg

Pinch of saffron threads, soaked in a little hot water for 10 minutes

### TO SERVE

Flatbreads

Boiled rice

1tsp paprika

50g whole blanched almonds, toasted

25g pine nuts, toasted

1tbsp chopped fresh chives or parsley

Mansaf is Jordan's national dish and it is always served on a big platter with local breads to celebrate special occasions or welcome visiting guests. Made with lamb, a good cut of meat is essential, and although Jordanians will usually cook the meat on the bone, boneless diced lamb can be used. Apart from the spices, there are only two main ingredients: lamb and jameed, a thick yoghurt made from goat's or sheep's milk.

### METHOD

Brown the lamb in batches in the oil or clarified butter in a large pan over a medium-high heat, removing the cubes of meat as they brown. When all the meat has been browned, add the onion to the pan and fry over a low heat until softened.

Add the coriander, cumin and cardamom and fry for 1 minute. Pour in the stock, return the lamb to the pan and bring to a simmer. Cover and cook gently for 1 hour 20 minutes or until the lamb is very tender. Remove any fat from the surface of the cooking liquid.

Whisk together the jameed or yoghurt, egg and a couple of tablespoons of the hot stock from the pan. Stir slowly into the pan, add the saffron and its soaking water and heat until the liquid is simmering gently.

> see tip

Cook, with the pan uncovered, over a low heat for 30 minutes, stirring occasionally.

To serve, arrange flatbreads over a large metal tray, covering it completely.

Spoon the boiled rice onto the flatbreads and the lamb on top, adding as much of the cooking liquid as you wish. Dust with paprika, sprinkle with the almonds and pine nuts, and scatter the chives or parsley over.

*Our Tip!* Once you've added the yoghurt mixture to the lamb, simmer it very gently because if the heat is too high the cooking liquid will split or curdle.

# ARABIC SALAD

## Jordanian side dish

**SERVES 2**

**PREPARE** 10 minutes

### INGREDIENTS

- ½ cucumber
- 2 large tomatoes
- 1 small onion, peeled
- 1 red or green chilli
- Small bunch of fresh coriander
- ½tsp salt
- Juice of 1 lemon
- Pinch of sumac

Exodus clients Mr and Mrs Murphy kindly donated this refreshing Jordanian salad as inspired by their travels together. The colourful ingredients need to be cut into similar-sized tiny dice and the salad is finished with a light dusting of sumac, a dark red, Middle Eastern spice with a sharp, lemony flavour.

### METHOD

Chop the cucumber, tomatoes and onion into small dice. Thinly slice the chilli and coarsely chop the coriander leaves.

Mix the diced vegetables and chilli together in a bowl and season with the salt. Pour over the lemon juice and toss until the ingredients are coated.

Spoon the salad into a serving dish or bowl, scatter over the coriander and sprinkle with the sumac.

# FALAFEL
## fried spiced chickpea balls

**MAKES about 20**     **PREPARE** 25 minutes (plus cooling and chilling time)     **COOKING** 20 minutes

### INGREDIENTS

2tbsp oil, plus extra for shallow or deep-frying

1 red onion, peeled and finely chopped

2 large cloves of garlic, peeled and finely chopped

1tsp ground cumin

2tsp ground coriander

1tsp paprika

400g can of chickpeas, drained and rinsed

400g can mixed beans, drained and rinsed

Finely grated zest of 2 limes or 1 lemon

1tbsp harissa

2tbsp plain flour

1 egg, beaten

### TAHINI & YOGHURT DIP

3tbsp tahini

6tbsp natural yoghurt

Juice of 1 lime

1tsp za'atar, for sprinkling

These crisp-coated balls are made from chickpeas, beans and spices. Exodus marketing director, Jae Hopkins, spent a year working in Sydney in the early 90s where the local takeaway did amazing falafel wraps...

'I tried to find something that compared when I got back to the UK, but never had any success,' she says. 'Move forward two decades and I found my deep-fried holy grail on a trip to Israel. A bit of pointing at ingredients and daft – if internationally recognisable – sign language later, and the lady in the backstreet café had explained the combination of chickpeas and beans, just the right mix of herbs, and that I needed to add lime zest – which is the key. Yum!'

### METHOD

Heat the oil in a small pan and fry the onion over a low heat until softened. Add the garlic, cumin, coriander and paprika and fry for a further 2–3 minutes, stirring frequently. Transfer to a large bowl and leave to cool.

Put the chickpeas and mixed beans in a food processor, add the lime or lemon zest, harissa, flour and beaten egg and whizz until smooth. Transfer to the bowl and mix with the onion and garlic.

Shape the mixture into balls, roughly the size of ping-pong balls, with damp hands and place on a large plate in a single layer. Chill for several hours to firm up.

Heat a couple of tablespoons of oil in a large frying pan for shallow-frying, or one-third fill a deep-fat fryer with oil and heat to 180°C. Shallow-fry the falafel a few at a time for about 10 minutes until golden brown and crisp all over, or deep-fry for 3–4 minutes. Drain on kitchen paper.

To make the dip, stir together the tahini and yoghurt and then mix in the lime juice. Spoon into a serving dish and sprinkle with the za'atar. Serve the falafel warm or cold with the dip.

*Our Tip!*     Za'atar is an aromatic Middle Eastern spice mix made from powdered dried hyssop leaves, sumac, toasted sesame seeds and salt. It is available in small pots or jars from larger supermarkets.

# HUMMUS

## creamy chickpea dip

PREPARE 10 minutes

### INGREDIENTS

400g can of chickpeas, drained and rinsed by running cold water through sieve

Juice of 1 lemon

3 or more (according to taste) fat garlic cloves, peeled and finely chopped

7tbsp tahini

About 5tbsp cold water

### TO SERVE

Olive oil

Chopped fresh coriander

Paprika

Flatbreads

This recipe is another favourite of Exodus marketing director, Jae Hopkins. 'The Exodus team tease me because I eat hummus almost every day for lunch in the office. I'm vegetarian and it's just such a great way to get some protein, as well as being totally delicious and easy to eat at my desk or take outside if the weather's good. My recipe is essentially one my mum got from a wholefood cookery course she did in the seventies but I added extra tahini after a guide I met in Israel extolled its virtues: he was right, of course!'

### METHOD

Put the drained chickpeas, lemon juice, chopped garlic, tahini and water into a food processor and blend to a purée.

Spoon the hummus onto a large plate and spread it out with the back of the spoon.

Drizzle with olive oil, scatter over chopped coriander and dust with paprika. Serve with flatbreads torn into pieces for scooping up the hummus.

*Our Tip!* If you make the hummus ahead you may find it thickens up on standing, so stir in extra cold water to bring it back to the right consistency. You can also sharpen the flavour with extra lemon juice.

# CHICKEN SHAWARMA

## pan-fried chicken wraps

| SERVES 6 | **PREPARE** 30 minutes (plus marinating time)   **COOKING** 4–6 minutes |

### INGREDIENTS

2 boneless chicken breasts, skinned

½tsp ground allspice

½tsp ground cinnamon

1tsp ground cardamom

1tsp ground cumin

1tsp ground coriander

½tsp freshly ground black pepper

3tbsp oil, plus extra for frying

3 cloves of garlic, peeled and crushed

Juice of 1 lime

### TO SERVE

4 large flatbreads, warmed

Finely chopped red onion and green pepper

Lime wedges

6tbsp tahini mixed with 2tbsp plain Greek yoghurt or 8tbsp hummus (see page 54)

The traditional way to roast meat for shawarma is on a revolving, vertical spit where joints of lamb, chicken, beef, veal and water buffalo are cooked slowly, often for up to a day. The meat is then thinly sliced and topped with tahini before being served on a plate or wrapped in a soft flatbread. As not many of us have a revolving spit in our kitchens, pan-frying the meat – in this case chicken – is a more practical way to cook a shawarma at home.

### METHOD

Place the chicken breasts between two sheets of cling film and beat with a rolling pin until thin.

Mix together the spices with the oil, garlic and lime juice and spread over both sides of the chicken breasts. Cover and leave in the fridge to marinate for several hours or overnight.

Heat a couple of tablespoons of oil in a heavy frying pan and fry the chicken breasts over a brisk heat for 2–3 minutes on each side until cooked through. Remove from the pan and cut into slices.

To serve, top the warmed flatbreads with the chicken and chopped red onion and green pepper. Squeeze over the juice from the lime wedges and spoon the tahini and yoghurt or hummus on top. Roll up or fold over the flatbreads and serve.

# COUSCOUS & FISH

## Tunisian speciality

| SERVES 4 |
|---|

**PREPARE** 20 minutes
**COOKING** about 30 minutes, plus standing time

### INGREDIENTS

600g monkfish fillet, cut into 2.5cm chunks

4tbsp plain flour

4tbsp olive oil

1 medium onion, peeled and thinly sliced

2 cloves of garlic, peeled and crushed

1 red pepper, deseeded and sliced

2tsp ground coriander

1tsp paprika

1 courgette, sliced

2tbsp sun-dried tomato purée

Juice of 1 lemon, plus extra lemon wedges to serve

1tsp hot chilli paste, e.g. harissa

Pinch of saffron threads, soaked in 2tbsp hot water for 15 minutes

400g can chickpeas, drained and rinsed

500ml fish or vegetable stock

50g raisins

300g couscous

Chopped broad leaf parsley, to garnish

Fish cooked with spices and served with couscous is a popular dish along Tunisia's Mediterranean coast. Any white fish with firm flesh can be used but monkfish works particularly well. With its fresh flavours and lightness, this is the perfect summer dinner party dish to share with friends.

### METHOD

Toss the monkfish chunks in the flour until coated. Heat half the oil in a large pan and fry the monkfish in batches over a fairly high heat until lightly golden, draining one batch from the pan onto a plate before you add the next.

When all the fish has been cooked, lower the heat under the pan and add the rest of the oil. Cook the onion until softened and then add the garlic, red pepper, coriander and paprika and fry for 5 minutes.

Add the courgette, tomato purée, lemon juice, chilli paste and saffron with its soaking water and stir over the heat for a couple of minutes.

Add the chickpeas, stock and raisins. Bring to the boil and stir in the couscous and monkfish. Cover the pan, remove from the heat and set aside for 5 minutes to give the couscous time to swell and absorb the stock.

Spoon into a serving dish, sprinkle with chopped parsley and accompany with lemon wedges to squeeze over.

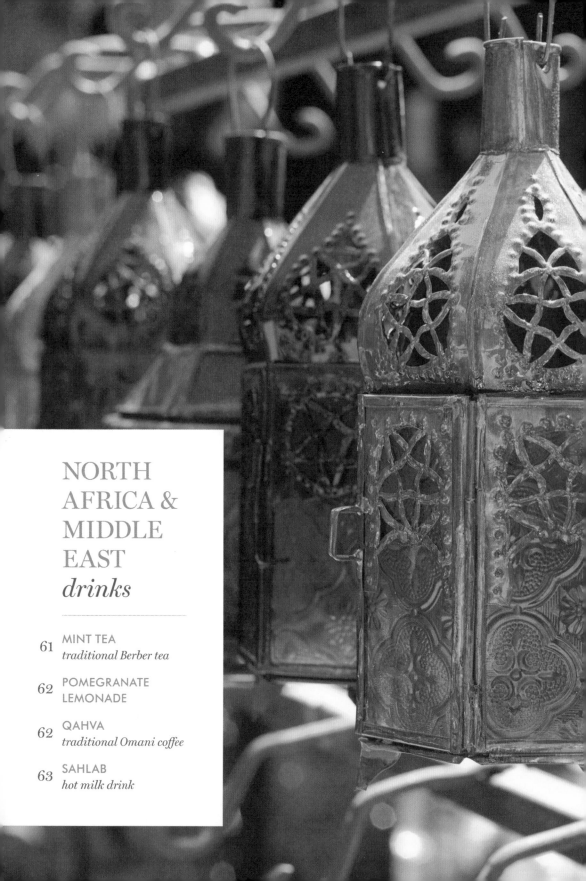

# NORTH
# AFRICA &
# MIDDLE
# EAST
## *drinks*

# MINT TEA
## traditional Berber tea

**SERVES 6**  |  **PREPARE** 10 minutes

Mint tea is served across the Maghreb countries of North Africa – Morocco, Algeria, Tunisia and Libya. Making and serving the tea has its own ritual and it is drunk throughout the day, being offered to guests to show they are welcome in the host's home, or to customers looking to purchase a carpet, jewellery or other item from the souks.

Exodus staff member Laura Frost recalls walking through the Atlas mountains on one of her first ever adventures and being welcomed by a local Berber family, 'We stepped out onto their roof terrace, and waiting for us was a cup of warm mint tea and a view of the mountains. That was the moment I fell in love with adventure travel.'

## INGREDIENTS

1tbsp loose Chinese gunpowder green tea

1 litre boiling water

3tbsp caster sugar, or to taste

Bunch of fresh spearmint leaves

## METHOD

Put the tea leaves in a warmed teapot and pour over the boiling water. Set aside to infuse for 2–3 minutes.

Stir in sugar to taste and add sprigs of fresh spearmint. Leave to infuse for a further 3–4 minutes.

Holding the teapot high, pour the tea through a fine strainer into small heatproof glasses and serve with a couple of extra fresh spearmint leaves in each glass.

# POMEGRANATE LEMONADE

**SERVES 4** | **PREPARE** 5 minutes

This long, cool drink is a favourite with staff member Gina Lawrence. 'The leathery-skinned pomegranate has been around since the dawn of time and some believe it was the fruit that tempted Eve in the Garden of Eden rather than the apple,' says Gina. 'Spike its beautiful ruby red juice with lemon, top it up with sparkling water and you've got a wonderfully refreshing drink for a hot day.'

### INGREDIENTS

3tbsp caster sugar, or to taste

Juice of 2 large lemons

300ml pomegranate juice

500ml sparkling mineral water

### TO SERVE

Crushed ice

Lemon slices

### METHOD

Put the sugar and lemon juice in a jug and stir until the sugar dissolves.

Add the pomegranate juice, stir well and then gradually pour in the sparkling water.

Add crushed ice and lemon slices to four glasses before filling with the pomegranate lemonade.

# QAHVA
## traditional Omani coffee

**SERVES 2** | **PREPARE** 5 minutes
**COOKING** 5 minutes
**STANDING TIME** 10 minutes

In the Gulf States, you'll rarely find qahva coffee in cafés as it is served in private homes to invited guests in much the same way that English people might have friends round for afternoon tea. Made from beans that have been high roasted to a rich dark brown, the coffee is quite bitter so is served with Arabic sweets or dates.

### METHOD

To make qahva coffee, add high-roast ground coffee and 1 tablespoon of ground cardamom to a pan of boiling water and boil for 3–4 minutes.

Remove the pan from the heat and leave the coffee to stand for 3–4 minutes.

Put whole cloves in a coffee pot and strain in the hot coffee. Leave to sit for 10 minutes, sweeten to taste and serve in small glasses.

# SAHLAB
## hot milk drink

**SERVES 2**   **PREPARE** 5 minutes   **COOKING** 10 minutes

Since ancient times this creamy drink has been made by simmering the ground tubers of a rare orchid – *Orchis macula* – with milk, and has been highly prized both as an aid to digestion and as an aphrodisiac. It is still possible to buy the powdered root in street markets but with the orchid in danger of becoming extinct, cornflour is now considered a more ethical alternative.

### INGREDIENTS

450ml milk

1½tbsp caster sugar

1tbsp cornflour

1tsp rose water

### TO SERVE

Ground cinnamon, to sprinkle

2tbsp finely chopped pistachios

### METHOD

Pour 50ml of the milk into a jug. Pour the rest into a saucepan and add the sugar.

Mix the cornflour with the milk in the jug, stirring until smooth and no lumps remain.

Heat the milk in the saucepan until it comes to the boil. Pour it into the jug, stirring or whisking constantly and then return the mixture to the pan.

Stir constantly over a low heat for about 5 minutes until the mixture is smooth and thickened.

› see tip

Remove the saucepan from the heat and stir in the rose water. Pour into two heatproof glasses and dust the tops with a little ground cinnamon. Sprinkle over the chopped pistachios and serve at once.

### Our Tip!

Make sure you stir the milk and cornflour mixture continuously as it comes to the boil to prevent any lumps forming. If it does begin to feel lumpy, remove the pan from the heat and stir or whisk briskly until the mixture is smooth again.

africa

# dishes

# NYAMA CHOMA
## roasted goat meat & salad

**SERVES 4-6**

**PREPARE** 30 minutes (plus marinating time)   **COOKING** about 15 minutes

### INGREDIENTS

3tbsp oil

Juice of 1 large lemon

2 cloves of garlic, peeled and crushed

2tsp curry powder

1tsp ground ginger

1tsp paprika

900g goat or beef meat, cut into 2.5cm chunks

### KACHUMBARI SALAD

1 red onion, peeled and thinly sliced or chopped

4 tomatoes, chopped

1 avocado, stoned, peeled and flesh cut into small chunks

1–2 red chillies, thinly sliced

Juice of 2 limes

Chopped leaf coriander

### UGALI

1 litre cold water

1tsp salt

225g white cornmeal (use millet flour if not available)

In Swahili, *nyama choma* means 'roasted meat' and it's a dish that is eaten all over East Africa from roadside food trucks in Tanzania to stylish restaurants in Kenya. Goat is the meat of choice as it is readily available and the fat it contains adds flavour as it roasts over the coals, but beef also works well. *Nyama choma* is eaten with the hands and usually accompanied with kachumbari salad and ugali.

### METHOD

In a bowl, whisk together the oil, lemon juice, crushed garlic, curry powder, ginger and paprika with a fork. Add the chunks of meat, stirring until they are coated. Cover and leave in the fridge to marinate for 1–2 hours or longer.

To make the salad, mix the onion, tomatoes, avocado and chillies together and squeeze over the lime juice. Spoon into a serving dish and scatter over some coarsely chopped leaf coriander.

Thread the chunks of meat onto skewers and roast over hot coals on a barbecue until cooked to your liking, turning the skewers over occasionally.

Alternatively, the meat can be cooked under a conventional grill.

While the meat is roasting, make the ugali. Bring the water and salt to the boil in a pan and slowly stir in the cornmeal. Cook over a medium heat, beating with a wooden spoon to remove any lumps, until the mixture has thickened, absorbed the water and leaves the sides of the pan – this will take about 10 minutes. Transfer to a bowl and form the mixture into balls with wet hands.

Serve the meat skewers with the salad and ugali.

# BOBOTIE

## spiced minced meat oven dish

| SERVES 4 |
|----------|

**PREPARE** 30 minutes (plus cooling time)   **COOKING** 25 minutes

### INGREDIENTS

2 onions, peeled and chopped

2tbsp oil

2 cloves of garlic, peeled and crushed

500g lean minced beef

2tbsp hot curry paste

1tsp dried mixed herbs

1tsp ground coriander

1tsp turmeric

2tbsp mango chutney

3tbsp sultanas

300ml beef stock

Salt and freshly ground black pepper

2 slices of white bread made into crumbs

300ml full-fat milk

2 large eggs

3 bay leaves

Client Linda Hill remembers 'I was travelling overland from Rwanda through Uganda and onto Kenya and our group stopped at a camp outside the Maasai Mara before our balloon flight. Bernard, our leader, cooked this dish for us and it was so good I now make it myself at home as it's become a favourite of my husband's.' The name of the recipe is pronounced 'ba-boor-tea' and it's South Africa's national dish.

### METHOD

Fry the onions in the oil in a large deep frying pan until softened. Add the garlic and minced beef and fry over a fairly brisk heat, breaking up any clumps of meat with a spoon, until the beef is browned.

Stir in the curry paste, herbs, ground coriander and turmeric and fry for 2–3 minutes, stirring frequently.

Add the chutney and sultanas and pour in the stock. Lower the heat, season and leave to simmer for 45 minutes, stirring occasionally.

Stir in the breadcrumbs and transfer the mixture to a shallow oven-proof dish, spreading the top level.

Preheat the oven to 180°C (fan 160°C)/gas 4. Beat together the milk, eggs and seasoning and pour over the meat mixture. Lay the bay leaves on top and bake for 35–40 minutes or until the topping is golden brown.

Serve hot.

# SESWAA

slow-cooked beef

**SERVES 6**

**PREPARE** 15 minutes **COOKING** about 5 hours

### INGREDIENTS

2tbsp oil

900g beef for slow cooking or casseroling, cut into large chunks

1 large onion, peeled and cut into wedges

4 bay leaves

Salt and freshly ground black pepper

Beef stock

A traditional dish from southern Africa that is packed with flavour but requires very few ingredients, just an inexpensive piece of beef designed for slow cooking, plus an onion, seasoning and bay leaves.

Seswaa is served with sadza, known as ugali in East Africa, a thick cornmeal porridge and a staple food of Botswana, plus a green vegetable such as these yard-long beans. As polenta is more readily available outside southern Africa, it makes a good alternative to sadza.

### METHOD

Preheat the oven to 150°C (fan 130°C)/gas 2. Heat the oil in a large cast-iron casserole dish and brown the chunks of beef on all sides.

Add the onion and bay leaves and season with salt and pepper. Pour over just enough beef stock to cover the beef and bring to the boil.

Cover with the lid and cook the beef in the oven for 4 hours. Transfer the casserole dish to the hob, remove the lid and simmer until almost all the cooking liquid has evaporated.

Crush the meat with a wooden spoon – it should fall apart easily – and serve with cornmeal porridge (see page 66) or soft polenta and a green vegetable.

# INJERA

## traditional flatbreads

| MAKES about 8 | PREPARE 10 minutes (plus standing time)  COOKING about 15 minutes |

### INGREDIENTS

7g sachet of fast-action
dried yeast

300g millet flour

600ml tepid water

⅛tsp bicarbonate of soda

In Ethiopia, these spongy flatbreads are not only for eating but used as a utensil to scoop up dishes like stew. Traditionally they would be made with teff flour, produced by grinding the seeds of teff grass very finely. The breads have a slightly spongy texture and, while teff flour can be difficult to track down outside of Ethiopia, they are equally good made with millet flour, which is available from health food stores.

### METHOD

Sprinkle the yeast over the flour in a large bowl. Gradually whisk in the water until smooth and you have a batter with the consistency of single cream. Cover the bowl and leave to stand at room temperature for 24 hours until frothy on top.

Add the bicarbonate of soda to the batter and stir it in.

Heat a non-stick frying pan. When hot, add a tablespoon of the batter, swirling the pan so the batter spreads out thinly over the base.

Cook for 1–2 minutes or until the flatbread has risen slightly and can be easily removed from the pan. It should be set underneath but not browned and slightly damp on top. Move to a plate and repeat the process until all the batter has been cooked.

# GINGER BEER CHICKEN

## campfire-inspired chicken casserole

| **SERVES 4** | **PREPARE** 20 minutes    **COOKING** about 45 minutes |
| --- | --- |

### INGREDIENTS

2tbsp oil

8 small chicken joints, such as drumsticks or thighs

1 large onion, peeled and finely chopped

1 can of minestrone soup

200ml ginger beer

100g mushrooms, sliced

Black pepper and a little salt, if required

75ml full-fat milk

2tsp plain flour

A little lemon juice, if required

Sprigs of thyme, to garnish

Exodus staff member Andy Gibbins brought this dish back from his Namibian cycling adventure. 'It was cooked for our group by Jonas, the assistant guide and chef – he did a fantastic job of keeping a bunch of hungry cyclists well fed. Everything he made was all freshly cooked on a campfire – inspiring!' he says.

'We were covering some long distances and Namibia doesn't have many shops outside the larger towns, so Jonas' ingenuity in creating different and tasty meals every night was amazing. One evening, sitting around a campfire after a day in the saddle, he presented us with ginger beer chicken and it was by far the most popular of all the delicious meals he prepared. It was so good I asked him for his recipe so I could share it with my friends when I got home.'

### METHOD

Place a flameproof casserole dish over a medium heat and add the oil. If the chicken joints have their skin on, brown them on all sides in the oil first and then drain from the pan. If the joints have been skinned you can skip this step and just add the chicken once the onion has been fried.

Add the onion to the casserole and fry until it softens and begins to turn brown.

Put the chicken in the casserole, pour in the minestrone soup and ginger beer and add the mushrooms. Season with black pepper and a little salt if necessary.

> *see tip*

Bring to the boil and simmer for 30 minutes or until the chicken is cooked through.

Lift the chicken joints out of the casserole and transfer them to a warmed serving dish. Stir the milk and flour together until smooth, add to the cooking juices in the pan and bring to the boil, stirring constantly.

Cook for 2 minutes and then taste the sauce. As some ginger beers are sweeter than others you may need to sharpen it with a little lemon juice. Pour the sauce over the chicken and serve at once with sprigs of thyme scattered over.

**Our Tip!**

If you're short of time, you can make the dish using boneless, skinless chicken thighs, cut into bite-size pieces. Add the chicken after you've fried the onion but before adding the soup and other ingredients – it will only need about 5 minutes cooking time.

# MATOKE
## Ugandan stew

**SERVES 4**    **PREPARE** 20 minutes    **COOKING** about 1 hour

This hearty stew takes its name from the green bananas or plantains known as matoke that are used to make it.

It is a national dish of Uganda, where plantains are a staple part of the local diet, and variations of the stew are made in other East African countries, such as Rwanda, Burundi and Tanzania.

### INGREDIENTS

3–4 green plantains, depending on size

> see tip

Juice of 1 lemon

2tbsp oil

1 large onion, peeled and finely chopped

500g lean minced beef

1 green pepper, deseeded and chopped

1 large red or green chilli, deseeded and finely chopped

1tbsp curry powder

1tsp ground coriander

1tsp ground cumin

4 tomatoes, peeled and chopped

300ml beef stock

3tbsp chopped fresh coriander

### METHOD

Peel the plantains and cut them into 2cm slices. Put the slices in a bowl and sprinkle with the lemon juice. Pour over boiling water to cover, set aside until the water feels cool and then drain.

Heat the oil in a large frying pan, add the onion and cook over a low heat until softened. Add the minced beef and fry until the meat browns, stirring frequently and breaking up any lumps with a spoon.

Add the green pepper and chilli and stir in the curry powder, coriander and cumin. Cook for a couple of minutes and then add the tomatoes and stock.

Bring to the boil, lower the heat under the pan and stir in the plantains. Cover the pan and simmer gently for about 45 minutes or until the plantains are tender and the meat is fragrant with the spices. Serve hot, sprinkled with chopped coriander.

### Our Tip!

Plantains are different from ordinary bananas in that they are larger, have pointed ends and are inedible raw. They can be found in African and Caribbean food shops and markets.

# SLAAI

avocado peanut salad

**SERVES 4 as a side dish**

**PREPARE** 10 minutes

## INGREDIENTS

2 large avocados

3tbsp lime or lemon juice

100g unroasted, unsalted peanuts

1tsp salt

1tsp grated root ginger

> see tip

The success of this simple traditional Swaziland salad depends on using perfectly ripe avocados and peanuts in their natural unroasted, unsalted state. Root ginger gives a touch of sweet spice, and freshly squeezed lime or lemon juice adds a citrusy tang. This is the perfect side salad accompaniment to a barbeque with friends and family.

### METHOD

Halve the avocados, remove the stones and peel away the skin. Chop the flesh into bite-size pieces and place in a bowl. Sprinkle over the lime or lemon juice and stir gently until the avocado pieces are coated.

Rub any skins off the peanuts with your fingers and chop coarsely.

Spoon the avocado and any lime or lemon juice left in the bowl into a serving dish, season with the salt and sprinkle over the ginger.

*Our Tip!* The quickest way to peel root ginger is using a teaspoon. Hold the spoon so the curve of the bowl is uppermost and drag it over the ginger from top to bottom to scrape away the skin – much easier than negotiating the root's knobbly crevasses with a knife.

# MOFO GASY

## risen little pancakes

**MAKES about 12**

**PREPARE** 15 minutes (plus rising time for batter)    **COOKING** about 10 minutes

### INGREDIENTS

60g plain or wholemeal  flour

50g rice flour

½tsp fast-action dried yeast

2tbsp caster sugar

175ml tepid water

2tsp condensed milk

½tsp vanilla extract

Oil or melted butter, for  greasing

Icing sugar, for dusting

The name of these round pancakes translates as 'Malagasy bread'. Made from a sweet yeast batter containing rice flour and condensed milk, the pancakes are cooked in a special pan with round holes into which the batter is spooned. Called an aebleskiver pan, it can be bought from specialist cook shops or online. Perfect for sharing with friends over coffee, after dinner or when you fancy a simple little treat!

### METHOD

Mix the flour, rice flour, yeast and 1 teaspoon of the sugar together in a bowl. Add the water, whisking until it is combined with the dry ingredients and you have a smooth batter.

Cover the bowl with cling film and leave in a warm place for 1 hour or longer, until the batter is risen and frothy.

Stir well and then mix in the rest of the sugar, the condensed milk and vanilla. Cover the bowl with cling film and leave the batter to rise again in  a warm place for about 45 minutes until frothy on top.

Heat an aebleskiver pan over a medium heat and grease the holes by brushing with a little oil or melted butter.

Spoon about a tablespoon of batter into each hole until it is filled and cook for a couple of minutes or until the bottoms of the pancakes are golden brown. Slide a small palette knife around the edge of each pancake to loosen it and then turn it over with two forks. Cook the other side until  golden brown.

Serve hot, dusted with icing sugar.

# ZAMBIAN BEEF

## beef stew pot

**SERVES 4**

**PREPARE** 30 minutes (plus marinating time)   **COOKING** about 1 hour 15 minutes

### INGREDIENTS

800g braising steak, cubed

2 cloves of garlic, peeled and chopped

2tsp paprika

Salt and freshly ground black pepper

2tbsp oil

2 onions, peeled and chopped

750ml beef stock

1tbsp chopped fresh rosemary leaves, plus extra to garnish

4 medium potatoes, peeled and cut into small chunks

2 carrots, chopped

2 sticks of celery, chopped

Slow-cooked beef dishes, where the meat and vegetables are gently simmered together over a low heat in one large pot, are a traditional part of East African cuisine. This dish was donated by Exodus customer Matthew Murphy, inspired by his travels.

### METHOD

In a large bowl, toss the cubes of beef with the garlic and paprika and season with salt and pepper. Cover and leave to marinate in the fridge for several hours.

Heat half the oil in a large pot and fry the beef in batches until browned, removing one batch from the pot before you add the next.

When all the beef has been browned, fry the onions in the pot over a low heat, adding a little more oil if necessary, until softened. Tip in the garlic from the bowl used to marinate the beef and fry until softened.

Return the beef to the pot, add the stock, rosemary, potatoes, carrots and celery and bring to the boil. Reduce the heat, cover the pan and simmer for 1 hour or until the beef and vegetables are tender.

# SAFARI CHICKEN

| SERVES 4 | PREPARE 20 minutes | COOKING 45 minutes |
| --- | --- | --- |

Jill Burns, a frequent Exodus traveller, recently joined us for a holiday in Kenya, Rwanda and Uganda. 'Ken was our cook on that trip,' she says, 'and he did a sterling job of feeding us all. I am not vegetarian but most of the dishes he produced, which I especially liked, were based around vegetables as, of course, he had to cook with limited resources. However, the following is one of my favourites and is quite versatile in that it can be cooked in a conventional oven, on a wood fire, or even on a gas hob or barbecue.'

## INGREDIENTS

1 butternut squash, peeled, seeds removed and reserved, and cut into thin slices

2–4 red chillies, depending on size, deseeded and finely chopped

1 tbsp chopped fresh rosemary

3 tbsp oil

4 boneless chicken breasts, skinned

100g goat's cheese, blue cheese or feta

Salt and freshly ground black pepper

50g butter, melted

Toasted seeds from the squash, to garnish

## METHOD

Spread out the slices of squash on a baking tray. Scatter with some of the chopped chillies and the rosemary. Drizzle with the oil and stir until the squash slices are coated.

Slit the chicken breasts open to make a pocket in each one. Divide the cheese into four equal pieces and push a piece into each pocket. Seal with small skewers or cocktail sticks.

Season the chicken breasts and brush them with the melted butter. Lay on top of the squash and seal the parcel tightly if cooking on a fire. If using an oven, cover the baking tray loosely with foil and cook in a 180°C (fan 160°C)/gas 4 for about 45 minutes or until chicken is cooked and the squash tender.

Towards the end of cooking, uncover the chicken and squash and sprinkle with the toasted seeds from the squash.

### Our Tip!

If feeding a crowd, you can make the dish go further by serving it with flatbreads. See page 71.

# AFRICA
*drinks*

# BUNNA COFFEE CEREMONY

om Harari visited Northern Ethiopia and had what he recalls as he best coffee I've ever had'. Although not a recipe, the ceremony etails how to create that special cup of dark nectar.

he coffee ceremony is a traditional part of the social and cultural fe of Ethiopians and being invited to attend such a ceremony is a nark of friendship and respect. An ancient proverb – *'Buna dabo aw'* – probably best explains the importance of coffee in Ethiopian fe – 'Coffee is our bread!'

he ceremony usually takes place three times a day – in the morning, t noon and in the evening – and it is the main social gathering vhen people meet to discuss important topics.

Vhile the ceremony varies slightly from one region to another, the nost widely practised is the 'Bunna' method, where the coffee-making quipment is set up on a piece of furniture that stands on a bed of cented long grasses and flowers and has a shelf called a 'rekbot'.

he hostess is generally dressed in a traditional white cotton thiopian garment with coloured designs woven along its edges. hey begin by roasting green coffee beans in a flat pan over a small harcoal or gas stove and the fragrance they give off mingles with he heady scent of frankincense and myrrh that are burned during he ceremony.

he hostess stirs the washed beans in the heated pan. As the beans ecome shiny and almost black, aromatic oils are released which erfume the room and the beans are then passed around for veryone to appreciate their powerful aroma. After being returned to he hostess, they are finely ground in a pestle and mortar and mixed vith spices before being brewed in a decorative clay pot called a ebena'. The shape of the pot allows the grounds to settle at the ottom and a narrow lip acts as a strainer to trap the grounds when he coffee is poured.

ouring is done in a thin, continuous stream with the pot held 30cm bove tiny cups called *'cini'*, a practice that takes years to perfect. he coffee or 'Bunna' is sweetened with plenty of sugar – or salt in ertain areas – and is often accompanied with small snacks. Three ounds are usually served: the first, known as 'Abol', being the trongest. The following two rounds are called 'Tona' and 'Baraka', vith the coffee becoming progressively weaker. Each of the three ounds is said to transform the spirit, the third being a blessing on hose who drink it.

normally drink my coffee with milk, even preferring a latte or appuccino, but this glass of sweetened black coffee could have onverted me, had this wonderful Ethiopian coffee been available to he every day.' says Tom.

# VANILLA MARTINI
## vodka-based cocktail

**SERVES 1**

**PREPARE** 5 minutes

You can have some fun with this snowy-white cocktail by dipping the rim of the glass in butterscotch or toffee dessert sauce before pouring in the drink. Choose a really thick sauce that clings to the rim of the glass and doesn't dribble down the sides and spoil the look of the martini.

### INGREDIENTS

Ice cubes

1 shot of Amarula cream liqueur

1 shot of vanilla vodka

2tbsp double or whipping cream

### TO SERVE

Butterscotch or toffee dessert sauce

Slice of star fruit

Small piece of vanilla pod (optional)

### METHOD

Three-quarters fill a cocktail shaker with ice cubes and add the Amarula, vodka and cream. Shake vigorously.

Pour some dessert sauce into a shallow dish and dip the rim of a martini glass in it.

Pour the martini into the glass and decorate by tucking a slice of star fruit over the rim and adding a small piece of vanilla pod, if you like. Serve at once.

*Our Tip!* Amarula is a cream liqueur made from the fruit of the South African Amarula or Elephant tree. When ripe, the fruits fall to the ground, begin to ferment and elephants find them irresistible. Whether they enjoy the resulting hangover as much has never been recorded.

# SPRINGBOK
## liquor shooter

**SERVES 1**          **PREPARE** 5 minutes

Also known as a Springbokkie, meaning 'little springbok' in Afrikaans. Downing one of these eye-catching shooters before dinner is a popular way to start a special night out in South Africa. The cocktail layers mirror the green and gold colours of the jerseys worn by the country's national rugby team, the Springboks.

### INGREDIENTS

25ml crème de menthe

25ml Amarula cream liqueur

### METHOD

Pour the crème de menthe very slowly over the back of a teaspoon into a shot glass, holding the teaspoon upright.

Repeat with the Amarula so it settles in an even layer on top of the crème de menthe. Serve at once.

# DAWA COCKTAIL
## vodka and honey cocktail

**SERVES 1**          **PREPARE** 5 minutes

Dawa means 'medicine' or 'magic potion' in Swahili and this potent cocktail reputedly cures anything that might ail you. Once the vodka has been added to the glass, the hand-carved tip of a wooden 'Dawa stick' is coated in set honey and used to muddle the ingredients together to bring out the lime's citrusy flavour and make the drink sweeter.

### INGREDIENTS

lime, cut into quarters

tsp brown sugar

Crushed ice

0ml vodka

et honey

### METHOD

Put the lime quarters into a glass and add the sugar.

Fill the glass with crushed ice and pour in the vodka.

Twist the end of a Dawa stick (or teaspoon) in set honey and put it in the cocktail. Use the stick to muddle the lime quarters with the sugar, honey and vodka. Serve immediately.

*asia*

# dishes

# PHO
## noodle soup

| **SERVES 4** as a main | **PREPARE** 15 minutes **COOKING** 20 minutes |

### INGREDIENTS

2 litres well-flavoured beef stock, bought or homemade

¼ star anise

1 black cardamom pod

4cm piece of cinnamon stick

2 whole cloves

1 tbsp Vietnamese fish sauce

50g piece of root ginger, skin on, grilled until browned

1 white onion, peeled, halved and grilled until browned

100g beansprouts

Small bunch of coriander leaves

4 small sprigs of Thai basil leaves

2 tbsp sliced papaya and shallot pickle

1 lime, cut into 8 wedges

500g cooked bánh pho rice noodles

350g cooked beef fillet, cut into thin slices

1 tbsp finely chopped peanuts

4 spring onion curls

> see tip

The recipe for this Vietnamese noodle soup comes from Exodus leader Phuong Tran. Pronounced 'Fuh', it consists of an aromatic and spicy broth to which thin, flat rice noodles called bánh pho are added, along with fresh herbs, bean sprouts and thin slices of meat – usually beef or chicken.

Phuong is from Hue, the former capital of Vietnam, a city famous not only for its old citadel, emperor tombs and monuments, but also for its food. Phuong has been with Exodus for almost 10 years and says the food trips he leads are his favourite. He sent us this recipe from one of his favourite restaurants in Loi An.

### METHOD

Bring the stock to the boil in a large pan, add the star anise, cardamom pod, cinnamon, cloves, fish sauce, grilled ginger and onion and simmer for 15 minutes. Strain through a fine sieve into another pan and return to the heat.

Blanch the beansprouts in hot water for 30 seconds and divide between four side plates with a few coriander leaves, the basil sprigs, papaya and shallot pickle and lime wedges.

Heat the rice noodles in a pan of hot water for 30 seconds, lift them out with a draining spoon and divide between four serving bowls.

Heat the slices of beef fillet in the same water for 5 seconds, lift out and add to the bowls. Ladle over the hot broth and garnish with shredded coriander leaves, finely chopped peanuts and spring onion curls. Serve the soup with the four side plates of accompaniments, so each person can add as much or as little as they want.

*Our Tip!* To make spring onion curls, trim spring onions and cut into 7-8cm lengths. Make cuts close together at one or both ends of the onions with a sharp knife and leave in a bowl of cold water in the fridge until the ends curl.

# FISH AMOK

## steam-cooked fish curry

| **SERVES 4** | **PREPARE** 30 minutes (plus cooling time)   **COOKING** 25 minutes |
| --- | --- |

### INGREDIENTS

2 red chillies, deseeded and chopped

3 cloves of garlic, peeled and coarsely chopped

1tsp turmeric

1tbsp grated root ginger

2 stalks of lemon grass, coarse outer layers removed and soft inner core sliced

4 kaffir lime leaves

2 banana shallots, peeled and chopped

Juice of 1 lime

2tsp shrimp paste

4tbsp palm sugar or soft light brown sugar

1tbsp oil

400g can of full-fat coconut milk

2 banana leaves

> see tip

500g fillet of firm white fish, such as haddock or cod, skinned and cut into 4 equal pieces

16–20 large raw prawns

### TO GARNISH

2 kaffir lime leaves, sliced into very fine strips

1 red chilli, sliced

Exodus traveller Alison Jarvis shares her Cambodian adventure – 'I first arrived in Cambodia in 2009 and fell in love with the country, its rich and unique culture, and its friendly, resourceful people. So much so that I stayed nearly seven years. Cambodia has its own very clearly identifiable cuisine, and fish amok would likely be on any visitor's hit list as one of the more popular dishes. It is very easy to find in local restaurants, from Malis to Romdeng to Khmer Surin to Knyay. Variations can be found with vegetarian and chicken options, but by far the most popular is the fish amok.'

### METHOD

Put the chillies, garlic, turmeric, ginger, lemon grass, lime leaves, shallots, lime juice, shrimp paste and sugar into a small food processor or pestle and mortar, and whizz or grind to a paste.

Heat the oil in a frying pan, add the paste and cook gently over a low heat, stirring frequently, until the paste smells fragrant. Reserve a little of the coconut milk for garnish and pour the rest into the pan. Bring to a simmer then remove the pan from the heat and leave to cool for 15 minutes.

Cut each banana leaf in half to make four rectangles. Fold up the sides of the rectangles to make 'dishes', holding the sides in place with cocktail sticks.

Divide the fish and prawns equally between the banana-leaf dishes and spoon over the coconut paste. Lift carefully into a steamer, cover and cook for 20 minutes or until the fish and prawns are opaque.

Transfer to serving plates, remove the cocktail sticks and spoon over the reserved coconut milk. Serve garnished with the strips of lime leaf and chilli slices. Accompany with steamed jasmine rice.

 *Our Tip!*

Banana leaves are available from Asian supermarkets but they are quite tricky to work with as they have a tendency to split along their ribs. To cook the dish completely in the frying pan, add the seafood after you've made the sauce and simmer gently until the fish and prawns turn opaque.

# ALOO GOBI

## dry spiced vegetable curry

| SERVES 2 | **PREPARE** 20 minutes (plus cooling time for potatoes)   **COOKING** 50 minutes |

## INGREDIENTS

3 medium potatoes

1 medium cauliflower

4–5tbsp oil

½tsp black mustard seeds

About 12 fenugreek seeds

½tsp cumin seeds

1tsp ground coriander

½tsp each of ground turmeric and ground cumin

1-2 dried red chillies

1 onion, peeled and finely chopped

1 fresh green chilli, finely chopped

4tbsp frozen peas (optional)

Salt, to taste

## TO GARNISH

Finely chopped fresh red chilli

2tbsp chopped fresh coriander

Shavings of fresh coconut

> see tip

The recipe for this dry vegetable curry comes from traveller Gaby Naylor who says, 'I have enjoyed cooking Indian food ever since I went to an evening class a number of years ago with my friend, Helen. My visit to India with Exodus was an amazing experience: the smells, the colours, the crazy traffic, the noise, the food, the beautiful architecture and, of course, the people. I enjoyed all the meals we had on the trip and came across so many different dishes during the week but this was one of my favourites. When I got home I couldn't wait to find a recipe and try it out on the same friend, Helen, who came for supper with her husband and another couple. Luckily, it went down very well!'

### METHOD

Boil the potatoes in their skins until just tender when pierced with a skewer. Drain, leave to cool completely and then peel and cut into chunks.

Blanch the cauliflower in a pan of boiling water for 2 minutes. Drain, cool and divide into small florets.

Heat the oil in a large shallow pan, add the mustard seeds and fry until they begin to pop. Add the fenugreek seeds, cumin seeds and ground spices, along with the dried red chillies, onion and green chilli. Stir well and fry over a low heat until the onion is soft and golden brown – about 10 minutes.

Add the cauliflower, cover the pan and cook for 5 minutes or until almost tender. Add the peas (if using) and potato chunks, season with salt and re-cover the pan. Cook for 10 minutes or until the potatoes are heated through.

Serve garnished with chopped red chilli and coriander leaves, plus shavings of fresh coconut.

*Our Tip!*   This recipe also works as a side dish, which serves 4.

# LOK LAK

## sautéed beef with dipping sauce

**SERVES 2**

**PREPARE** 25 minutes (plus marinating time)   **COOKING** 5 minutes

## INGREDIENTS

300g rump or sirloin steak, cut into thin strips

2tbsp groundnut oil

### MARINADE

2tbsp dark soy sauce

1tbsp oyster sauce

1tbsp tomato purée

2 cloves of garlic, peeled and crushed

### SALAD

Shredded lettuce

Tomato slices

Cucumber slices

### DIPPING SAUCE

Juice of 2 limes

2tbsp cold water

1tsp brown sugar

1tsp fish sauce

1tsp freshly ground black pepper

Traveller Gyan Fernando visited Thailand, Laos and Cambodia with us in April 2012. 'In Cambodia I was not expecting anything different by way of food because in this region the cuisines, although spicy and delicious, have a sameness. I had not been to Kampuchea before and in a waterfront restaurant called the Veiyo Tonle, in Phnom Penh, sitting with the group for dinner, I came across Beef Lok Lak. As soon as I tasted it I loved it and continued to find it in other towns. I managed to work out the recipe and have recreated it in my own home in rural Devon. I've also passed it on to my sisters in Sri Lanka, who later visited Kampuchea and enjoyed it as well!'

### METHOD

Mix the marinade ingredients together until evenly blended.

Put the strips of beef in a bowl, add the marinade and stir until the strips are coated. Cover and chill in the fridge overnight so the beef absorbs the flavours of the marinade.

Heat the oil in a wok or large frying pan. Lift the beef out of the marinade and stir-fry over a high heat for 3–4 minutes or until browned. Pour in the marinade left in the bowl and stir over the heat for 1 minute so the beef is coated.

Arrange the salad ingredients on a serving plate. Mix the ingredients for the dipping sauce together and pour into a small bowl.

Spoon the beef on top of the salad, serve with the dipping sauce and accompany with boiled or steamed rice.

# TEMPURA
## vegetables in light batter

| SERVES 4 | PREPARE 15 minutes   COOKING 15 minutes |
|---|---|

**BATTER**

2 egg yolks

300ml chilled water

200g plain flour

½tsp ground ginger

**TEMPURA**

1 cauliflower, divided into small florets

Groundnut oil for deep frying

1 red pepper, deseeded and cut into 8 wedges

1 orange pepper, deseeded and cut into 8 wedges

Exodus staff member Jack Gamble tried tempura when he first met his Japanese sister-in-law, who wanted to cook for him and his family as a thank you for their hospitality. Since then, he's tried and tested lots of different types of tempura with her recipe, but cauliflower and pepper are now his favourite. 'They have the best crunch on the outside but softness when fried – perfect with the light Japanese batter.'

These vegetable fritters have a light, crisp coating and are perfect for sharing. Serve them with small bowls of soy sauce infused with shredded ginger and sweet chilli sauce, for dipping. Great for vegetarians, although you can replace vegetables with ingredients like prawns.

### METHOD

To make the batter, whisk the egg yolks and water together in a bowl, until frothy. Sift in the flour and ginger and whisk until just mixed in. The batter should have the consistency of single cream, so add a little more water if it is too thick.

To prepare the tempura, blanch the cauliflower florets in a pan of boiling water for 2 minutes, or until almost tender. Drain.

Heat the oil to 190°C. Using chopsticks or tongs, dip the cauliflower florets and pepper wedges one at a time into the batter and fry in batches of 6–8 pieces for 3–4 minutes or until they are pale golden and crisp.

Drain the fritters on kitchen paper in a single layer as they cook, and keep warm in a low oven. Serve them hot with dipping sauces.

*Our Tip!* It's important to heat the oil to the correct temperature, as if it's too hot the fritters will burn before they're cooked in the middle, and if it's too cold they'll absorb a lot of oil and become soggy. If you don't have a deep-fryer with a thermostat, inexpensive cooking thermometers can be bought from kitchen shops or online.

# LARB

## spicy minced pork salad

| SERVES 4 | PREPARE 15 minutes    COOKING 6 minutes |
|---|---|

### INGREDIENTS

2 stems of lemon grass, white part only

2 fresh green chillies, deseeded

1 tbsp oil

500g lean minced pork

50ml fresh lime juice

Grated zest of 1 lime

2–6tsp chilli sauce (depending on how hot you want the dish to be)

Shredded lettuce

3tbsp roughly chopped leaf coriander

2tbsp small fresh mint leaves

1 small red onion, peeled and very finely chopped

40g roasted peanuts, chopped

2tbsp crisp fried garlic

Thailand is synonymous with street food and curries, but Thai Larb salad (usually minced pork or chicken) is unusual, perfect for food on the go, healthy and light but with a slight kick. Dan Jackson, Exodus stalwart, says 'I first tried it on the streets of Chiang Mai, needing some fuel to garner the energy for another assault on the famous night market. It's perfect with an ice-cold Singha.'

### METHOD

Slice the white part of the lemon grass across the stems as finely as possible. Finely chop the green chillies.

Heat the oil in a wok or large frying pan. Add the lemon grass, chillies and pork mince and stir-fry for 6 minutes over a high heat, breaking up any lumps of mince with your spoon, until the meat is browned and cooked through.

Tip the mince mixture into a bowl and leave it to cool.

Add the lime juice, zest and chilli sauce, stirring it into the mince until combined.

Arrange shredded lettuce over a serving plate. Stir most of the chopped coriander, mint, onion, peanuts and fried garlic through the mince and spoon it over the lettuce.

Sprinkle the remaining herb leaves, onion, peanuts and garlic on top and serve.

# KASHK BADEMJAN

## aubergine stew

| SERVES 4 | **PREPARE** 15 minutes  **COOKING** 30 minutes |
|---|---|

### INGREDIENTS

3tbsp olive oil

3 aubergines, peeled and thinly sliced

1 large onion, peeled and thinly sliced

4 cloves of garlic, peeled and finely chopped

1tsp turmeric

2tbsp dried mint

2tbsp kashk, Greek yoghurt or full-fat soured cream

Salt and freshly ground black pepper

### TO GARNISH

2tbsp coarsely chopped walnuts

Small fresh mint leaves

Tom Harari of Exodus says, 'Aubergine is the Iranian potato, and aubergine stew in various forms is very popular all over Iran. Without doubt, the best one we had was in the troglodyte village of Maymand. People have lived in the cave dwellings there for a long time and a few still live in them today. After exploring the village we were invited to one of the dwellings for lunch. Laid out on a rug on the floor were bowls of the most delicious aubergine stew. We all agreed it was the best meal we had in our two weeks travelling around Iran.'

### METHOD

Heat 2 tablespoons of oil in a large frying pan and when really hot, add the aubergine slices and fry until they have softened and are turning golden. Drain the slices from the pan onto a plate lined with kitchen paper.

Add the remaining tablespoon of oil to the pan, lower the heat and fry the onion until softened. Add the garlic and turmeric and fry for a further 5 minutes. Remove the pan from the heat and stir in the dried mint. Reserve a spoonful of the onion mixture for garnish.

Mash or blend the aubergine to a purée. Add the purée to the frying pan and stir into the onion mixture with the kashk (or yoghurt or soured cream, if using) and dried mint. Season with salt and freshly ground black pepper.

Return the pan to a low heat to warm everything through. Spoon into a serving dish and scatter the chopped walnuts, mint leaves and reserved onion mix over the top. Serve as a light meal or as a dip with flatbreads.

# BEETROOT CURRY

| **SERVES 4** as a side | **PREPARE** 15 minutes   **COOKING** 20 minutes |

## INGREDIENTS

500g raw beetroot, tops and bottoms trimmed but unpeeled

> see tip

1tbsp oil

1tsp black mustard seeds

1tsp fenugreek seeds

8–10 fresh curry leaves

1 medium onion, peeled and finely chopped

3 green bird's eye chillies, slit in half lengthways

1tsp chilli powder

125ml coconut milk

Salt

Beetroot might not be the first vegetable that comes to mind when you think of curry but don't just take our word for it – beetroot cooked with spices and coconut milk is absolutely mind blowing. Sri Lankans like their food explosively hot, with chillies featuring in practically every recipe, even ones served at breakfast. So if your taste buds are less robust, reduce the amount you add accordingly.

Elise Wortley of Exodus, on a whistlestop tour of Sri Lanka, tried many Sri Lankan curries 'for breakfast, lunch and dinner!' but by far the beetroot curry was her favourite. Here she shares the recipe she brought home: 'it's really simple, I'm not that great at cooking and even I could make it!'

## METHOD

Put the whole beetroot in a saucepan and cover with cold water. Bring to the boil, lower the heat and simmer for about 30 minutes or until the beetroot are tender. Drain and set aside to cool.

Peel the cooked beetroot and cut into bite-size pieces. Heat the oil in a pan, add the mustard seeds and fenugreek seeds and fry until the spices are fragrant.

Add the onion, green chillies and chilli powder and stir until the onion and chillies are coated in the spices.

Add the beetroot and coconut milk and stir. Season with salt and simmer gently for 10 minutes. Spoon into a serving dish and serve as a side dish with rice and other curries.

*Our Tip!*   It's important not to tear the skins of the raw beetroot as their vivid red juice will leak out into the water when the beetroot cook and they'll lose their flavour. If you wash your hands well immediately after peeling the beetroot stains disappear completely... a bit of lemon juice also works wonders.

# THUKPA

## Nepalese noodle soup

| | |
|---|---|
| **SERVES 4** | **PREPARE** 15 minutes   **COOKING** about 15 minutes |

### INGREDIENTS

3tbsp vegetable oil

1 red onion, peeled and thinly sliced

1 tomato, sliced

1 carrot, cut into matchsticks

3 cloves of garlic, peeled and finely chopped

1tbsp grated root ginger

1 litre boiling water

½tsp salt

200g pak choi, roughly chopped

100g dried egg noodles

Soy sauce, to taste

Here at Exodus, we know that travel can change your perspective on life. Frequent travellers Derek and Carol Darke found that out after a few weeks holiday with Exodus to Kerala and then Ladakh. Their trip was such a success that when they returned home they gave up their jobs and set off on a 13-month adventure to explore Sri Lanka, India and Nepal.

'We first encountered this soup on holiday in Tibet, and were thrilled to discover its popularity in Nepal. One evening we left our guest house in Kathmandu and discovered a cafe down a small bustling side street where the locals ate. We were served bowls of a steaming clear soup with vegetables and noodles which we recognised straightaway as the Thukpa we had enjoyed so much previously.

'We were so impressed with the freshness of the ingredients and the abundance of spices in Asia that on our return to the UK, after much experimentation, we launched our own spice company!'

### METHOD

Heat the oil in a large saucepan, add the onion, tomato, carrot, garlic and ginger and fry for 5 minutes until the vegetables soften.

Pour the boiling water into the pan, add the salt and bring back to the boil.

Add the pak choi and noodles and simmer until the noodles are soft. Add soy sauce to taste and serve ladled into bowls.

### GO * SPICE

'Having experimented with many recipes and enjoyed meals cooked with our own freshly prepared spices, our company Go Spice Mixes Ltd was born. Our aim is to create as many spice blends based on cuisines from as many countries around the world as we can. We currently have 20 different blends, with others coming soon!'
– Derek Darke.

You can visit their site at www.gospice.co.uk

# GIMBAP
## seaweed rice rolls

| SERVES 6 | PREPARE 45 minutes (plus standing time)<br>COOKING 8 minutes |
|---|---|

First cousin to Japanese sushi, Korean gimbap or kimbap is the country's favourite light lunch or snack. Made by rolling steamed white rice (bap) and sheets of dried seaweed (gim or kim) around a variety of fillings, the rolls are then cut into thin slices before eating. As well as making gimbap to be enjoyed every day, skilled chefs are transforming it into works of art, creating tiered wedding cakes or arranging fillings as pandas, faces or flowers.

### INGREDIENTS

300g white short grain rice

1tbsp soy sauce

1tsp sesame oil

1tsp salt

5–6 sheets of dried laver seaweed

### SUGGESTED FILLINGS

fish such as:
tuna or salmon

cooked meat such as:
beef or pork

### OTHER SUGGESTIONS

raw carrots or daikon (white radish), cooked spinach, boiled eggs, cucumber

### METHOD

Put the rice in a sieve and run cold water through it until the water is clear. Drain well and put in a saucepan. Add 330ml of boiling water, cover and simmer gently for 8 minutes. Turn off the heat, cover the pan and leave the rice to stand for 15 minutes.

Add the soy sauce, sesame oil and salt to the hot rice and stir. Transfer the rice to a shallow dish and turn it over with a spatula until it has cooled a little – it should still be warm.

Place a sheet of seaweed on a sushi mat and spread the surface with an even layer of rice. Add your chosen fillings, chopped or shredded into small strips or chunks as necessary, and roll the seaweed sheet around the rice and fillings, dampening the final edge to stick it down.

Repeat with the remaining seaweed sheets, rice and fillings to make more rolls. Cut the rolls into slices using a sharp knife, dampening the blade first.

# WARM DUCK SALAD
## with soy dressing

| SERVES 4 |
| --- |

**PREPARE** 30 minutes    **COOKING** 15-30 minutes

### DRESSING

2tbsp dark soy sauce

1tsp finely grated root ginger

1tbsp clear honey

Dash of balsamic vinegar

Pinch of chilli flakes

### SALAD

2 large duck breasts, skin on

Salt and freshly ground black pepper

100g bag of watercress

2 small oranges, peeled and cut into segments, or replace one of the oranges with 6 cherry tomatoes, halved

6–8 spring onions, trimmed and roughly chopped

50g walnut halves

Having travelled to China a few years ago, Exodus staff member Olly Pemberton shares this dish inspired by his experiences. 'Duck is a major ingredient in Chinese cuisine and this dish is perfect for a light summery meal.' Enjoy as a starter for 4 people.

### METHOD

Mix the dressing ingredients together. Set aside for the flavours to infuse until ready to serve.

Preheat the oven to 200°C (fan 180°C)/gas 6. Score the skin of the duck breasts with a sharp knife and season.

Heat an ovenproof frying pan and when very hot, lay the duck breasts in the pan skin side down. Fry over a high heat for 4–5 minutes then transfer the pan to the oven and cook for a further 10 minutes for pink, or 15–20 minutes for well done.

Rinse the watercress and pat dry. Arrange on serving plates with the oranges and cherry tomato halves, if using, and chopped spring onions.

Remove the duck from the oven and leave to rest for 3 minutes. Drain the breasts from the frying pan and cut into thin strips using a sharp knife across the grain of the meat to ensure it stays meltingly tender.

Arrange the duck over the salad ingredients and drizzle with some of the dressing. Scatter over the walnuts and serve with the remaining dressing for diners to add more if they wish.

# KHAO SOI

## curried chicken noodle soup

| SERVES 4 | PREPARE 20 minutes  COOKING 20 minutes |
| --- | --- |

### INGREDIENTS

3tbsp red Thai curry paste

1tbsp mild curry powder

400ml chicken stock

25g palm sugar

2tbsp Thai fish sauce

500g boneless chicken thighs, skinned and cut into bite-size pieces

300ml full-fat coconut milk

50g beansprouts

300g dried egg noodles

Groundnut oil, for shallow-frying

### TO GARNISH

2 spring onions, trimmed and sliced

1 red onion, peeled and finely chopped

Coriander leaves

Lime wedges

> see tip

Exodus traveller Jasmin Roman has fond memories of this curried noodle soup from north Thailand. 'About 8 years ago I went to Chiang Mai as part of a very short trip to Thailand. I can remember sitting down at an outdoor seating area by a temple and letting my friend pick out a dish at random for me. She chose Khao Soi, telling me it was a 'must have' dish from the region. Due to dietary limitations, I'm generally not adventurous with food but this dish was amazing – extremely flavourful and just perfect.'

### METHOD

Heat a wok or large frying pan, add the curry paste and curry powder and fry for a couple of minutes until they become fragrant. Pour in the stock and bring to the boil.

Add the palm sugar, fish sauce, chicken, coconut milk and beansprouts. Lower the heat and simmer for 15 minutes or until the chicken is cooked.

Meanwhile, bring a saucepan of water to the boil, drop in the noodles and cook for 4–6 minutes or until tender.

Heat oil for shallow-frying in another wok or frying pan. Drain the noodles thoroughly and divide three-quarters of them between four warmed soup bowls. Fry the remainder over a brisk heat until crisp and golden, stirring frequently. Drain onto a plate lined with kitchen paper and, when cool enough to handle, break into short lengths.

Ladle the curry into the soup bowls over the noodles and sprinkle with the spring onions, red onion and coriander leaves. Pile the crisp noodles on top and serve with lime wedges to squeeze over.

 *Our Tip!* Take care to pat dry the noodles being fried with kitchen paper to remove any water clinging to them. If they are still wet when you add them to the hot oil, the oil will spit.

# ASIA
## *drinks*

# MANGO LASSI
## yoghurt-based drink

**SERVES 2** | **PREPARE** 10 minutes

Few foods taste as sublime as a ripe mango and, for connoisseurs, the finest mango of all is India's small, voluptuously shaped Alphonso. In season for just a couple of months each year during late spring and early summer, Alphonso mangoes have deep gold, honeyed flesh and are truly the fruit of kings – or perhaps that should be maharajas.

### INGREDIENTS

250ml plain yoghurt

150ml full-fat milk

200g peeled mango flesh, chopped

2tsp sugar, or to taste

Ground cardamom or ginger, for sprinkling

### METHOD

Put the yoghurt, full-fat milk, mango flesh and sugar in a liquidiser and blend until smooth and creamy.

Pour into tall glasses and sprinkle with ground cardamom or ginger. Serve at once.

> 66
>
> There was nothing more refreshing than escaping the heat of Rajasthan for a traditional mango lassi – it was my favourite drink from my travels! – Jenny Cox
>
> 99

# ARRACK COCKTAIL
## spirit distilled from coconut flowers

**SERVES 1**

**PREPARE** 5 minutes

Not to be confused with the grape-based spirits of the Middle East known as arak or raki, Ceylon arrack is made from the flower of the coconut palm. Nimble young climbers, known as Toddy Tappers, scale the trees wielding fearsome machetes to slash the flowers and release their sap. As soon as it is collected, the sap begins to ferment, prior to it being distilled and then aged to produce the island's local spirit.

### INGREDIENTS

Ice cubes

50ml Ceylon arrack

150ml ginger beer

Lime wedge

Mint sprig, to serve

### METHOD

Fill a highball glass with ice cubes and pour in the arrack.

Add the ginger beer, followed by a squeeze of lime juice.

Serve at once, decorated with a sprig of fresh mint.

## ASIA • VIETNAM

# CÀ PHÊ DÁ

## iced coffee

**SERVES 2** | **PREPARE** 10 minutes

Known locally as cà phê dá or café da, this traditional Vietnamese iced coffee is made from locally grown beans that have been dark-roasted and coarsely ground. Each cup is brewed in an individual French-style drip filter before being poured over sweetened condensed milk and served over ice. It can also be made by infusing the coffee grounds in a jug of boiling water, filtering it into a heatproof glass and stirring in the condensed milk.

### INGREDIENTS

4tbsp dark roast ground coffee

450ml water

4tbsp sweetened condensed milk

Ice cubes

### METHOD

Brew the coffee with the water using either a drip filter machine, or in a jug and then pouring it through a filter paper or fine strainer.

Divide the condensed milk equally between two cups, pour in the hot coffee and stir until the milk dissolves and mixes with the coffee.

Add ice cubes to two tall glasses and pour in the hot milky coffee, stirring briskly with a spoon.

# BOBA

## bubble tea

**SERVES 1** | **PREPARE** 15 minutes

This long, cooling, tea-based drink gets its name from the tapioca pearls dropped into the glass that sink to the bottom where they form an intriguing layer of 'bubbles'. If tapioca reminds you too much of school dinners, you could replace the pearls with tiny cubes of jelly.

The tea can be served plain or flavoured with fruit extracts.

### INGREDIENTS

2tbsp dried milk powder

1tbsp caster sugar or sugar syrup (or to taste)

150ml hot black tea

Ice cubes

1tbsp cooked tapioca pearls

1tsp natural fruit flavouring, eg melon, blueberry, cherry or raspberry (optional)

### METHOD

Put the milk powder, sugar or sugar syrup and hot tea into a jug and stir until the milk powder and sugar have dissolved.

Pour the mixture into a cocktail shaker or other container with a screw-top, add plenty of ice cubes and shake vigorously until frothy.

Put the tapioca pearls into a tall glass and strain in the tea.

Add a few ice cubes and serve with a wide straw to suck both the tea and tapioca through as you drink. Add optional flavouring.

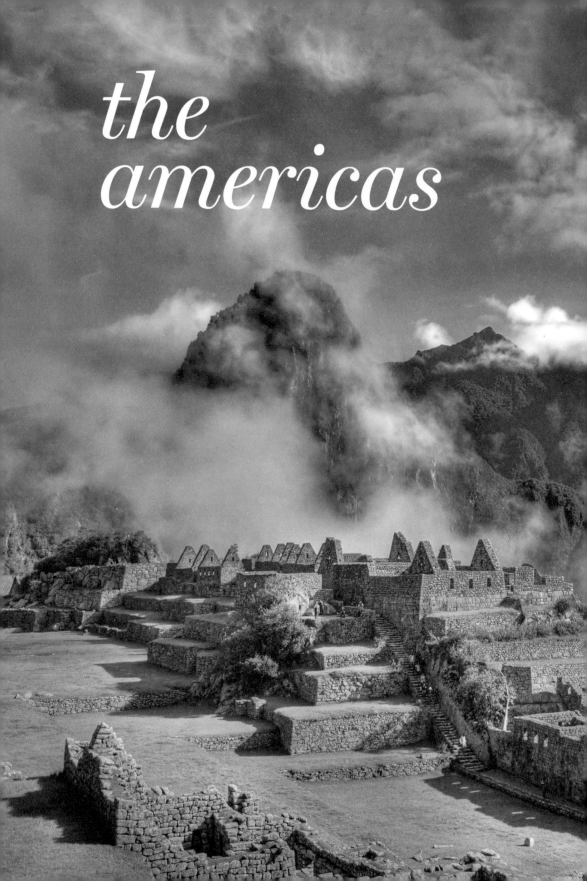

# the
# americas

# dishes

# LOMO SALTADO

## Peruvian stir-fry

**SERVES 2**

**PREPARE** 20 minutes  **COOKING** about 15 minutes

### INGREDIENTS

1 large potato

Vegetable oil for deep frying (preferably sunflower or rapeseed)

2 beef tenderloin steaks, sliced into strips about 4cm  long

Salt and freshly ground  black pepper

1 medium onion, peeled  and sliced

½ medium-sized red  pepper, deseeded and  sliced

1 aji amarillo chilli, cut  into  thin slices

> see tip

2 cloves of garlic, peeled and finely chopped

2tbsp soy sauce

2tbsp white wine or cider  vinegar

Handful of flat leaf parsley, roughly chopped, plus a few extra leaves for garnish

Tim Fearn of Exodus explains why he has fond memories of this dish. 'In 1995, I went to study in Peru, which was the first time I'd spent longer than a couple of weeks outside the UK. The year I spent in South America instilled a love of travel in me. Being a student on limited funds, I was always on the lookout for ways to live as cheaply as possible and eating with the locals in the market in Cuzco was a great way to save money. This dish was a particular favourite and every time I cook it, I'm reminded of sitting on wooden seats in front of rows of stalls that served up amazing-tasting food on battered tin plates, surrounded by an incredible variety of fresh local produce and the constant buzz of activity.'

### METHOD

Peel the potato and cut into thin but quite wide chips. Heat oil for deep-frying and fry the chips until golden brown and crisp. Drain from the pan onto a plate lined with kitchen paper.

Season the strips of steak with salt and pepper.

Add a tablespoon of the oil used for cooking the chips to a wok, and when really hot, add the steak and stir-fry for about 2 minutes over a brisk heat so it browns quickly and the juices are sealed inside. Drain the meat from the wok and set aside.

Add another tablespoon of the oil to the wok and stir-fry the onion, red pepper and chilli with a pinch of salt for 2–3 minutes. Add the garlic, soy sauce and vinegar and return the meat to the pan.

Stir well, taste and adjust the seasoning if necessary, and then add the chopped parsley and chips. Cook for a further 1 minute until the chips are  hot.

Transfer to serving plates and garnish with a few parsley leaves. Accompany with white rice.

*Our Tip!*  The aji amarillo chilli has been grown in Peru since the time of the Incas and is the country's most popular variety. 'If it is unavailable,' says Tim, 'a serrano chilli can be used instead.'

# TAMALES
## steamed corn-based wrap

**MAKES about 16**

PREPARE 1 hour (plus soaking for dried husks and cooling time)
COOKING 2 hours (for the meat filling), 45 minutes (for the tamales)

Tamales have their origins in Latin America and date back to the time of the Aztec and Mayan civilisations. Back then, wrapping the fillings in corn husks to create neat parcels made tamales the perfect portable food for travellers or armies and today they are still a favourite snack for busy people on the move. The filling is made in two parts, one a dough using masa harina (maize flour) and the other a mix of meat, vegetables, fruit or cheese.

### INGREDIENTS

Dried or fresh corn husks

### FOR THE MEAT FILLING

500g boneless lean pork (shoulder or leg), cut into 4 or 5 pieces

1 large onion, peeled and cut into wedges

2 cloves of garlic, peeled and finely chopped

600ml chicken or vegetable stock

2tbsp chilli sauce, plus extra to serve

1 large tomato, deseeded and finely chopped

2tbsp sweetcorn kernels

### FOR THE DOUGH

150g white vegetable fat

300g masa harina

Pinch of salt

1tsp baking powder

### METHOD

If using dried corn husks, soak them in a large bowl of water for 2 hours. If using fresh, there is no need to soak them.

To make the meat filling, put the pork in a large pan, add the onion, garlic and stock and bring to the boil. Lower the heat, cover the pan and simmer for 2 hours or until the meat is very tender.

When the pork is cooked, lift the pieces out of the pan, place in a bowl and shred with two forks. Strain the cooking liquid and reserve 300ml (the rest can be used for another recipe). Stir in the chilli sauce, tomato and corn kernels and leave both the meat and the reserved stock to cool.

To make the dough, beat the white vegetable fat until it is smooth and soft. Gradually beat in the masa harina, salt and baking powder, a little at a time, alternately with the reserved 300ml of cooking liquid.

Pat the corn husks dry, if necessary. Lay one husk on a board with the smaller end pointing away from you. Spread 2–3 tablespoons of the dough thinly over the husk to within 2.5cm of the edges. Top with 1–2 tablespoons of the meat filling.

Fold in the sides of the husk over the filling and roll up. Tie with thin string to make a parcel. Repeat with the remaining husks, dough and meat filling.

Stand the parcels upright in a steamer and steam for 45 minutes. Serve hot, snipping off the string with scissors and peeling away the husks. Top with extra chilli sauce to serve.

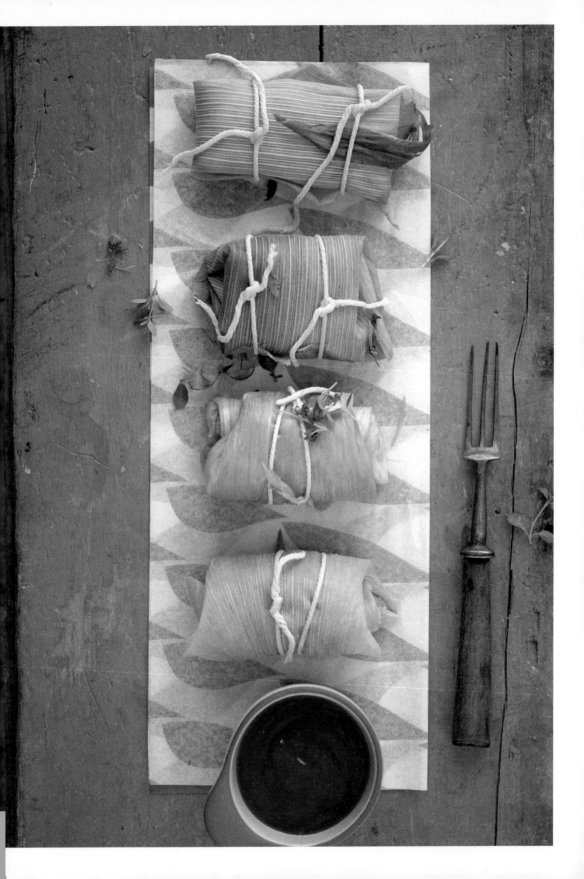

# SALT COD

## Caribbean fish dish

| | |
|---|---|
| **SERVES 4** | **PREPARE** 30 minutes (plus soaking time for cod)   **COOKING** about 50 minutes |

### INGREDIENTS

600g salt cod

4 green figs/green
unripe bananas

2tbsp oil

1 medium onion, peeled
and sliced

3 cloves of garlic, peeled
and crushed

¼ small Scotch bonnet
chilli pepper, deseeded and
finely chopped

> see tip

4 large green cabbage leaves,
finely shredded

2 tomatoes, cut into wedges

Sprigs of fresh thyme, to serve

The beautiful Caribbean island of St Lucia is famous for its fish dishes as well as its liberal use of blazingly hot Scotch bonnet peppers. Salt cod is used to make this colourful pan-fry, which is as vibrant as the island itself, and combines the fish and peppers with finely shredded cabbage, tomatoes and green unripe bananas, known as 'green fig'.

### METHOD

Rinse the salt cod under cold running water. Place in a bowl, cover with cold water and leave to soak for 24–36 hours, changing the water regularly. The fish needs to be soaked for this length of time so its flesh rehydrates and excess curing salt is removed. Drain the fish and rinse again under running water.

Slit the bananas down their length with the point of a sharp knife. Trim off the ends and place the whole bananas in a saucepan. Bring to the boil and cook for 20 minutes, during which time the banana skins will darken.

Drain and cool before peeling off the banana skins and cutting the bananas into 2cm lengths.

Simmer the cod in a pan of hot water for about 5 minutes or until cooked. Drain and separate the flesh into large flakes.

Heat the oil in a large frying pan and fry the banana slices until golden on both sides. Remove from the pan, add the onion and fry for 10 minutes or until softened and turning brown. Add the garlic and chilli, frying for 2–3 minutes. Add the shredded cabbage and a couple of tablespoons of water to the pan and fry for 3–4 minutes or until the water evaporates and the cabbage is just tender.

Add the tomato wedges and salt cod and return the fried banana slices to the pan. Cook for about 5 minutes, stirring occasionally but taking care not to break up the fish. Serve hot with thyme sprigs scattered over.

*Our Tip!*

Take extra care when preparing chillies, especially Scotch bonnets, which weigh in at an impressive – but scary – 100,000–350,000 units on the Scoville scale. It's not the chilli flesh that gives nasty burns but the membranes inside holding the seeds in place. Prepare chillies wearing thin disposable gloves or use a knife and fork to prevent your fingers coming into contact with them.

# PORK CARNITAS
## pulled pork tacos

**SERVES 8**

**PREPARE** 20 minutes (plus overnight marinating)   **COOKING** 4–5 hours

## INGREDIENTS

1.5kg boned pork shoulder, trimmed of fat and cut into 6 chunks

24 corn taco shells or flour tortillas, warmed in the oven

### MARINADE

1 onion, peeled and finely chopped

3 cloves of garlic, peeled and finely chopped or crushed

2tbsp hot chilli sauce

3tbsp tomato purée

200ml fresh orange juice

75ml lime juice

3tbsp white wine vinegar

2tsp dried thyme or oregano

2tsp ground coriander

2tsp ground cumin

### ACCOMPANIMENTS

Shredded lettuce

Chopped tomatoes

Finely chopped red onion

Coriander

Hot chilli sauce

Lime wedges

Soured cream

Mexican street food is becoming increasingly popular, with restaurants, pop-ups and festival food vans all jumping on this culinary bandwagon. And we've jumped too. We love delving into the cuisine and culture of a destination – and Mexico certainly doesn't disappoint.

Messy to assemble and even messier to eat, it's no surprise tacos are popular with all ages. A great do-it-yourself dish if you have friends round and don't want to spend ages in the kitchen. Once you've cooked and shredded the pork you can just leave everyone to help themselves to their chosen fillings. They can be served with flour tortillas or corn tacos depending on what you can find in your local supermarket.

### METHOD

Put the chunks of pork in a casserole dish. Mix all the marinade ingredients together and pour over the pork. Leave the pork to marinate overnight in the fridge.

Preheat the oven to 150°C (fan 130°C)/gas 2. Cover the casserole dish with a sheet of foil and the lid, and cook in the oven for 4–5 hours or until the pork is very tender.

Lift the chunks of pork out of the casserole dish and shred the meat. Spoon it into a serving bowl and drizzle with a few tablespoons of the cooking liquid.

Spoon the accompaniments into separate bowls and pile the warm taco shells onto a serving plate. Place everything on the table and leave diners to fill the tacos themselves.

# FEIJOADA
## black bean stew

**PREPARE** 30 minutes    **COOKING** 4 hours, or longer

### INGREDIENTS

2tbsp oil

150g bacon lardons

3 chorizo sausages, cut into bite-size pieces

700g pork shoulder steaks, cut into 2.5cm chunks

3 medium onions, peeled and chopped

4 garlic cloves, peeled and finely chopped

2tsp dried chilli flakes

About 900ml chicken stock

2 bay leaves

2tbsp white wine vinegar

400g can black beans, drained and rinsed

This slow-simmered stew of black beans and pork is popular in former Portuguese colonies around the world such as Macau, Angola, Goa, Mozambique and, of course, Brazil. It's a great standby dish if you have a crowd to feed as, once all the ingredients are in the pot, you can leave the stew to cook slowly for several hours without worrying about it spoiling or needing any last-minute attention.

'I remember it so clearly, because it was one of my favourite days,' recalls Emma Garrick of Exodus. 'It was after visiting Poço Azul, an underground pool with the most incredible, quite unnatural-looking blue waters. After moving on to the next town my friends and I shared a big black bean stew whilst talking about how amazing the day had been.'

### METHOD

Heat the oil in a large frying pan and cook the lardons over a medium heat until they are golden. Drain from the pan and transfer to a casserole dish.

Add the chorizo pieces to the pan and fry until they are evenly coloured. Drain from the pan and add to the casserole dish.

Fry the chunks of pork in the frying pan in batches over a brisk heat, stirring them frequently so they brown evenly all over. As one batch browns, drain and transfer it to the casserole dish before adding the next.

Lower the heat under the frying pan, add the onions and fry gently until softened. Add the garlic cloves and chilli flakes and continue to cook until the onions are golden. Transfer to the casserole dish.

Preheat the oven to 140°C (fan 120°C)/gas 1. Pour enough stock into the casserole dish to cover the meat, and add the bay leaves and vinegar. Cover the casserole dish with a sheet of foil and a lid, and cook in the oven for 2 hours.

Add the drained black beans to the casserole dish, stirring them into the sauce, and top up with more stock if necessary. Replace the foil and lid and cook for a further 1 hour or until the meat is meltingly tender. Serve with rice, hot chilli sauce and leaf coriander.

# CEVICHE

## fresh fish marinated in citrus juices

| **SERVES 8** | **PREPARE** 20 minutes (plus chilling time 1 hour) |
| --- | --- |

### INGREDIENTS

500g very fresh white fish fillet such as halibut, snapper or monkfish

Salt

Pinch of ground cumin

2 aji limo (habanero) chillies, deseeded and finely chopped or sliced

6 sprigs of leaf coriander, chopped (stalks and leaves)

Juice of 10 limes

1 red onion, peeled and finely sliced or chopped

### TO SERVE

6 pitted green olives, finely chopped

Shavings of avocado or chopped lettuce

2 plum tomatoes, peeled, deseeded and chopped

Many of us at Exodus, and our local partner in Peru, Gary Cohen, are big fans of ceviche. Gary explains, 'Mochica was a flourishing kingdom on what is now the north coast of Peru from the 1st to the 8th century, and its inhabitants used to eat raw fish with chillies, particularly the 'limo' chilli, which they cultivated. When the Spanish arrived in Lima, they brought with them a Moorish recipe based on fish, onions and limes, and the two were gradually combined to become 'ceviche', the most famous dish in modern Peru.'

And don't let the thought of raw fish put you off – the citrus juices will 'cook' the fish whilst it marinates, creating a deliciously fresh appetizer. Trust us, this is a delightful little recipe to share with friends.

### METHOD

Rinse the fish and pat dry with kitchen paper. Cut it into cubes measuring about 3 x 2cm, keeping them as uniform as possible. Spread out in a shallow dish and sprinkle with salt, a pinch of cumin, the chopped chillies and the coriander.

Spoon the lime juice over the fish, carefully turning the cubes so they are evenly coated with salt and juice.

Refrigerate the fish for at least 1 hour or overnight. The fish will 'cook' in the acidic marinade and become opaque. Put the chopped onion in a small bowl, cover and chill along with the fish.

When ready to serve, remove both the fish and the chopped onion from the fridge. Lift the fish from its marinade and place on a serving dish. Scatter over the chopped onion and garnish with the chopped green olives, avocado shavings or chopped lettuce, and chopped tomatoes. Spoon over a couple of tablespoons of the marinade and serve at once.

 *Our Tip!* To extract the maximum amount of juice from a lime, roll the lime around on the work surface with your hand before cutting it in half or quarters. This loosens the membranes inside the lime that hold the flesh in place so, when squeezed, the juice runs out more freely.

# CHIMICHURRI

## dipping sauce

**PREPARE** 15 minutes

### INGREDIENTS

3tbsp finely chopped fresh flat leaf parsley

2tbsp finely chopped fresh oregano

2–4 cloves of garlic, according to taste, peeled and crushed

4 spring onions, trimmed and finely chopped

1 small, medium-heat, red chilli, deseeded, ribs inside removed and finely chopped, or 1–2tsp dried chilli flakes

2tbsp red wine vinegar

1tbsp freshly squeezed lemon juice

50ml olive oil

Salt and freshly ground black pepper

Exodus traveller Haydn McCarthy admits he's an unashamed carnivore and has always had a soft spot for a steak. 'For years, I always went for a classic peppercorn sauce but my first visit to Argentina changed all that. In a basement restaurant in Buenos Aires, I ordered a tenderloin with chips and a bottle of Malbec (for the princely sum of US$5!). When the perfectly cooked steak arrived, the only accompaniment was a small dish of green sauce. Not knowing what it was, I put a small amount on the first piece of meat and the taste was phenomenal, it really brought out the flavour of the steak. Now this is the only sauce I make if I cook steaks at home, and everyone I know who's been to Argentina has been bitten by the chimichurri bug.'

### METHOD

Combine all the ingredients in a bowl, mixing well.

Taste and adjust the flavour if desired, adding extra herbs, garlic, chilli, lemon juice or seasoning.

The chimichurri can be refrigerated for up to 48 hours but it is best served as soon as it is made.

# PEPIÁN

## chicken stew

**SERVES 4**

**PREPARE** 1 hour   **COOKING** about 1½ hours

## INGREDIENTS

8 chicken thighs or 4 chicken breasts, skin on

½ cinnamon stick

1tbsp allspice berries

6 whole cloves

6 whole black peppercorns

1tbsp coriander seeds

1tbsp chilli flakes

2tbsp pumpkin seeds

1tbsp sesame seeds

2tsp dried oregano

1tbsp oil

1 medium onion, peeled and quartered

6 plum tomatoes

3 cloves of garlic, peeled

750ml chicken stock

1tbsp cornflour or masa harina

2 large potatoes, peeled and cut into small chunks

½ butternut squash, peeled, deseeded and cut into small chunks

Salt and freshly ground black pepper

Coriander leaves, to garnish

This spicy meat stew is one of Guatemala's oldest dishes and is a fusion of Mayan and Spanish cuisines. Thick and rich, its bold flavours come from spices, seeds and vegetables that are roasted until aromatic, before being puréed together. Popular as street food, Pepián is usually served with rice or corn tortillas.

### METHOD

Grill or roast the chicken pieces until cooked.

While the chicken is cooking, heat the cinnamon stick, allspice berries, cloves, peppercorns and coriander seeds in a dry heavy frying pan over a medium heat until they smell fragrant. Transfer to a bowl.

Add the chilli flakes, pumpkin seeds, sesame seeds and oregano to the frying pan and toast these until the sesame seeds are golden. Transfer all the spices and seeds to a mini processor or grinder and blitz to a powder.

Heat the oil in the frying pan, add the onion quarters, whole plum tomatoes and garlic cloves, and cook them over a medium heat until the onion and garlic are golden and the tomatoes scorched on all sides. Remove from the pan. Strip the skins off the tomatoes and coarsely chop the flesh.

Tip the ground spices and vegetables into a food processor or blender, add 150ml of the stock and blitz until smooth. Pour into a large pan, and stir in all but a couple of tablespoons of the remaining stock.

Mix this reserved stock with the cornflour or masa harina until smooth and stir it into the pan. Bring to the boil, stirring constantly until the mixture has thickened a little and is smooth. Add the chicken, potatoes and squash to the pan, lower the heat, cover the pan and simmer for about 30 minutes or until the vegetables are tender. Adjust the seasoning if necessary.

Serve hot with coriander leaves scattered over, and accompanied with boiled rice or corn tortillas.

# THE AMERICAS
*drinks*

# MOJITO
## white rum highball cocktail

**SERVES 1** | **PREPARE** 5 minutes

Exodus traveller Caroline Flatley donated her recipe for the perfect Cuban mojito, as taught to her by a casa particular (Cuban homestay) owner in the Bay of Pigs on a recent cycling trip. She says she's replicated it at home – 'it's brilliant and very easy to do. Drink it outside on a warm evening in Cuba with salsa music playing in the background. Failing that', she assures us, 'it still has the required effect on a back patio in Oldham.'

## INGREDIENTS

Generous handful of fresh mint leaves, plus extra to serve

2 limes, plus extra wedges to serve

4 heaped teaspoons of caster sugar

Ice cubes or crushed ice

A double measure of white Cuban rum

Soda water

A splash of Angostura bitters

## METHOD

Put half the mint leaves in the bottom of a highball glass and muddle them until bruised but still intact – this will release the mint's herby fragrance.

Squeeze the juice from the limes into the glass and add the sugar. Stir until mixed and the sugar dissolves.

Add two or three ice cubes or crushed ice. Pour in the white rum and top up with a splash of soda water. Drizzle a few drops of bitters on top.

Serve with extra lime wedges dropped into the glass and mint sprigs. Drink with a straw.

# THE HURRICANE
## classic New Orleans cocktail

**SERVES 1** | **PREPARE** 5 minutes

Relative to the daquiri, this passion fruit rum-based cocktail is enjoyed in the Caribbean and New Orleans.

Most of the islands have their own hurricane cocktail mixes and, in the 1940s, Pat O'Brien, a tavern owner in New Orleans, invented one for the city. Shaking together a potent mix of rum, orange juice and passion fruit juice, and served in hurricane lamp shaped glasses, it proved an instant success and is still the tipple-of-choice in the bars of the French Quarter today.

### INGREDIENTS

100ml white rum (or 50ml white and 50ml dark rum)

50ml orange juice

Juice of 1 lime

50ml passion fruit juice

1tbsp sugar syrup

Crushed ice

1tbsp grenadine

Orange slices, to serve

### METHOD

Put the rum, orange juice, lime juice, passion fruit juice and sugar syrup in a cocktail shaker and shake vigorously.

Fill a tall glass with crushed ice and pour in the contents of the shaker.

Add the grenadine and serve with a couple of orange slices.

# BATIDO
## Colombian smoothie

**SERVES 2**

**PREPARE** 5 minutes

This Colombian smoothie is made with luscious fresh papaya. Its sweet orange flesh is sharpened with a squeeze of lime and it is just the thing to kick-start your day.

### INGREDIENTS

Crushed ice

175g fresh papaya flesh, cut into chunks, plus extra wedges to serve

350ml milk

1tbsp lime juice

4tbsp sugar, or to taste

### METHOD

One-quarter fill a blender goblet with crushed ice and add the papaya flesh, milk, lime juice and sugar.

Blitz everything together until smooth and pour into glasses.

Decorate with papaya wedges and serve immediately.

# PISCO SOUR
## Chilean grape brandy cocktail

**SERVES 1**

**PREPARE** 5 minutes

taff member Adam Roberts had his first pisco sour in 2012 after moving Chile. 'Chileans drink huge quantities of pisco (distilled grape brandy) nd love visitors to do the same. This exotic drink is strong, but now a rm favourite of mine. And if ever in Southern Patagonia, try the purple alafate sours made from local berries.'

### IGREDIENTS

e cubes or crushed ice

egg white

)ml Chilean Pisco

ml sugar syrup

bsp freshly-squeezed lemon
   lime juice

op of Angostura bitters

### METHOD

Fill a cocktail shaker with ice cubes or crushed ice.

Put the egg white, Pisco, sugar syrup and lemon or lime juice in the shaker. Cover and shake for 15 seconds.

Strain into an Old Fashioned cocktail glass or tumbler and top with a drop of bitters.

*recipe index*

# RECIPE INDEX

## A

## B

## C

# THANK YOU

The Exodus cookbook has been an idea floated by both customers and the team at Exodus HQ for many years. We're very pleased now to have made that idea a reality, but we couldn't have done it without all our wonderful contributors...

First and foremost, we'd like to say a massive thank you to the customers who contributed their favourite recipes, stories from their travels, and of course, time. And to those who wrote back just to encourage us to do it, and said you were looking forward to seeing the result. Your responses made it possible.

We'd particularly like to send a heartfelt thank you to Mr & Mrs Murphy, Linda Hill, Jill Burns, Alison Jarvis, Gaby Naylor, Gyan Fernando,

Carol and Derek Darke of Go Spice, Jasmin Roman, and Caroline Flatley – thank you so much for sharing your knowledge with us.

We would also like to take this chance to thank our knowledgeable and passionate leaders and partners all around the world. Without you, our trips would not be the same, and nor would this cookbook. We're especially grateful to Austrian tour leader Bob Mason, the Acampora brothers from Hotel Due Torri in Italy, Exodus local partners Mark and Carey Faulkner in Chamonix, all at Cortijo Rosario in Spain; Vietnamese leader Phuong Tran, and Gary Cohen our local partner in Peru – for your knowledge, time and recipes. You've helped bring this cookbook alive.

We would also like to thank those at Exodus HQ who were able to spare their time to tell us their own travel tales and recipe recollections. Thank you to: Gina Eckersley, Louis Millington, Marta Marinelli, Dan Jackson, Jae Hopkins, Gina Lawrence, Andy Gibbins, Tom Harari, Jack Gamble, Elise Wortley, Tim Fearn, Emma Garrick, Jenny Cox and Adam Roberts. And an extra special thank you to Laura Frost and Emma King – your creativity, time and dedication brought this project to life.

To all our customers – whether you've contributed to this book, or not – you inspire us. Thank you for trusting us to take you around the world. That's what keeps us going, keeps us striving to create the best adventure holidays on the planet.

Last but not least, we'd like to thank you for reading this cookbook. We hope that the recipes inside its pages help to bring back memories or enable you to make new ones, whether it's by cooking with friends and family, or by inspiring you to travel and delve into a new culture, and of course, cuisine. Because really, that's what it's all about.

## FOLLOW EXODUS TRAVELS

 www.exodus.co.uk / www.exodustravels.com

 www.instagram.com/exodustravels

**f** www.facebook.com/exodustravels

🐦 @exodustravels

▶ www.youtube.com/user/exodustravels

'Once the travel bug bites there is no known antidote, and I know that I shall be happily infected until the end of my life.'

– Michael Palin

3 5 7 9 10 8 6 4 2

Ebury Press, an imprint of Ebury Publishing,
20 Vauxhall Bridge Road,
London SW1V 2SA

Ebury Press is part of the Penguin Random House group of
companies whose addresses can be found at
global.penguinrandomhouse.com

Penguin
Random House
UK

First published by Exodus Travels in 2016
This edition published by Ebury Press in 2017

Food photography © Ian Garlick
Publisher & Art Direction: Laura Frost
Lead Design: Emma King
Design: Hanna Michalak
Recipe Editorial: Wendy Sweetser
Food Stylist: Wendy Sweetser
Proofing & Index: Aune Butt and Helena Caldon
Copy writer: Gina Lawrence
Travel photography: Exodus Travels, Thinkstock and
Shutterstock

www.eburypublishing.co.uk

A CIP catalogue record for this book is available from the
British Library

ISBN 9781785037245

Printed and bound in China by C&C Offset Printing Co., Ltd

**MIX**
Paper from
responsible sources
FSC® C018179